ACCIDENTS

IN NORTH AMERICAN MOUNTAINEERING

VOLUME 10 · NUMBER 3 · ISSUE 66

2013

the
**AMERICAN
ALPINE club**

AMERICAN ALPINE CLUB

ALPINE

Marc Beverly

© 2013 The American Alpine Club

ISSN: 0065-082X
ISBN: 978-1-933056-81-4
ISBN (e-book): 978-1-933056-82-1

Manufactured in the United States ♻ Printed on recycled paper

Published by:
The American Alpine Club
710 Tenth Street, Suite 100
Golden, CO 80401
www.americanalpineclub.org

COVER IMAGES:

[Front] Simul-rappelling from the summit of Sister Superior, a sandstone tower in Castle Valley, Utah. *Andrew Burr*

[Back] Rescue on Mt. Bancroft in the Front Range, Colorado. See report on page 52. *Adam Pérou Hermans, courtesy of Alpine Rescue Team*

[Next page] Flight For Life, Rocky Mountain Rescue Group, and Rocky Mountain National Park rangers rescue an injured climber below the Diamond on Longs Peak, CO. *Flight For Life*

CONTENTS

MASTHEAD

THE AMERICAN ALPINE CLUB

SAFETY ADVISORY COUNCIL 2013
Aram Attarian, John Dill (NPS Ranger, Yosemite National Park), Chris Harder (NPS Ranger, Grand Teton National Park), Jeff Sheetz (Portland Mountain Rescue), and John E. (Jed) Williamson (Chair)

MANAGING EDITOR
John E. (Jed) Williamson

ASSOCIATE EDITOR
Aram Attarian

COPY EDITORS
Joe Forrester, Erik Hansen,
Dougald MacDonald

KNOW THE ROPES CONTRIBUTORS
Mike Poborsky (IFMGA/AMGA) and Rick Weber

LAYOUT
Erik Rieger

ADDITIONAL THANKS
David Boersma, Erik Lambert, Adam McFarren, Benjamin Pontecorvo

THE ALPINE CLUB OF CANADA

Ernst M. Bergmann
Chair, Safety Committee
safety@alpineclubofcanada.ca

Robert Chisnall
Canadian Content Editor
anam@alpineclubofcanada.ca

PREFACE

The Sixty-Sixth Annual Issue of
Accidents in North American Mountaineering

CANADA:

We thank Canada for submitting reports from Alberta and British Columbia for this year. Robert Chisnall, an ACC member from Kinsgston, Ontario, was responsible for editing the narratives.

UNITED STATES:

This is the second year for a new section in *Accidents* called "Know the Ropes: Fundamentals to Save Your Life," which targets common causes of many of the incidents analyzed herein. We hope these technical tips will increase awareness and education, and thus help prevent accidents. The topic for this year is lowering, which seems especially appropriate given that, since 2003, there have been 79 reported errors in this category.

Unfortunately, rappel errors, the topic of last year's Know the Ropes section, continue to be a frequent contributor to incidents. Whereas the average number of rappel errors over a 10-year period was seven per year, there were 17 incidents reported this year. We'll assume that our tips did not capture a wide enough audience of climbers.

This year we have grouped accidents by climbing centers in each state rather than by date. The goal is to help readers understand the trends in significant locations. We are no longer listing all mountain rescue teams in the U.S., primarily because the website of the Mountain Rescue Association contains this and much more information. We encourage you to visit this site: www.mra.org.

Aram Attarian continues his much-valued contributions as ANAM associate editor, collecting narratives and data from the Southeast and Colorado. In addition to the AAC professional staff, Erik Hansen and Joe Forrester continue their contributions as copy editors.

Along with the dedicated individuals on the Safety Advisory Council, we are grateful to the National Park Service rangers who forward their incident reports, and to all individuals who send in or post their personal stories.

JOHN E. (JED) WILLIAMSON
Managing Editor
7 River Ridge Road
Hanover, NH 03755
jedwmsn@mac.com

RESCUE COVERAGE

THE AMERICAN ALPINE CLUB'S RESCUE BENEFITS

Since 1947, the American Alpine Club has published *Accidents in North American Mountaineering* annually, helping you prevent accidents on your own. But prevention isn't the only answer for coming out of a crisis alive.

Even when using great judgment, no one is immune to accidents. Whether you're close to home or climbing on a faraway expedition, AAC rescue coverage provides peace of mind in case something goes wrong.

Members of the American Alpine Club are automatically enrolled for $10,000 of rescue benefits that pay for out-of-pocket costs in the United States as well as Global Rescue services internationally. These services get used regularly. In 2012 alone, 20 AAC members were rescued in the U.S., Nepal, Argentina, France, and Switzerland.

COVERAGE DETAILS

Global Rescue ($5,000) — This benefit covers you anywhere in the world for rescue and evacuation by or under the direction of Global Rescue personnel. If you're injured beyond the trailhead, no matter the elevation, we will come to your aid. Members who want more than $5,000 of coverage can upgrade at a 5% discount by visiting *americanalpineclub.org/rescue*. **HOW TO USE THIS BENEFIT**: Call +1 (617) 459-4200 as soon as possible during an emergency.

Domestic Rescue ($5,000) — This benefit reimburses AAC members for out-of-pocket rescue costs in the United States. This benefit can be used in addition to the Global Rescue service. **HOW TO USE THIS BENEFIT**: File a claim within 30 days of evacuation by calling (303) 384-0110 or emailing claims@americanalpineclub.org. We will send you a check.

Activities covered include climbing, hiking, backcountry skiing, mountain biking and more—if it's human-powered on land and you're rescued, you're covered.

JOIN THE AMERICAN ALPINE CLUB

americanalpineclub.org/join
(303) 384-0110

Only active members may use these services. Immediately gain access to your $10,000 of rescue coverage by joining the American Alpine Club. As a member you also will be supporting the publication of this book, and you'll receive free copies of the latest *Accidents in North American Mountaineering* and *American Alpine Journal*, among many other benefits.

Don't leave yourself hanging.
RESCUE HAS NEVER BEEN EASIER.

americanalpineclub.org/rescue

Menno Boermans

KNOW THE ROPES: LOWERING

FUNDAMENTALS TO SAVE YOUR LIFE

By Mike Poborsky, UIAGM/IFMGA
Graphics By Rick Weber

L owering a climbing partner is among the most common situations leading to injuries and rescues reported in *Accidents in North American Mountaineering*, whether it's lowering a climber after she tops out on a sport route or a partner in difficulty on a multi-pitch climb. In this year's Know the Ropes section, we will look at common causes of accidents related to lowering, and provide some best practices for preventing them.

Why is it so important to have a good understanding of lowering skills and techniques? Think about how often we lower a climbing partner. We all do it frequently in single-pitch climbing, whether top-roping, gym climbing, or lowering the leader after he finishes a sport, ice, or traditional route. We tend to emphasize the belaying aspect of these activities, when in fact data shows there is substantial risk of an accident occurring during the lowering phase. Think about it in these terms: If all goes well during the climb, we don't even use the safety systems in place. They are simply there "just in case" the climber falls. Once the lowering process starts, however, every component in the system engages and is critical to the safety of the climber. Then, of course, there are unlimited scenarios in multi-pitch climbing—whether rock, alpine, or ice—where lowering can be an

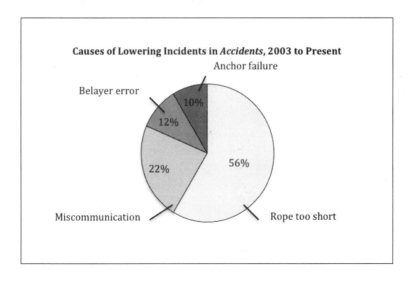

Causes of Lowering Incidents in *Accidents*, 2003 to Present

effective tool to increase the speed of the party or to help a frightened or incapacitated partner.

Based on the incidents reported in *Accidents* over the past decade, the four most common causes of lowering accidents are: a rope that's too short, miscommunication, an inadequate belay, and anchor failure. We'll look at each of these issues and provide basic and advanced skills and techniques to address some of these common problems. Regardless of whether we are lowering from below or above, or are in single or multi-pitch terrain, many of the same skills and techniques are required.

Rope Too Short

More than half of all lowering accidents reported in *Accidents* in the past decade occurred when the rope end shot through a belay device and the climber fell uncontrollably. It is very easy to misjudge the length of your rope and/or the height of the anchor in vertical terrain. However, most of these unfortunate accidents could have been prevented simply by closing the system. This will make it impossible for the rope to unintentionally pass through the belay device.

In a typical single-pitch climbing scenario, where the pitch length is less than half the available rope, the ground closes the system by default, meaning your partner is going to make it back to the ground before the belayer gets to the end of the rope, so closing the system is unnecessary. The problem comes when the anchor is near or above the midpoint of the typical rope. This is increasingly common as new routes are established with anchors above 30 meters (half the typical modern rope length). For some climbs, a 70-meter rope is now mandatory to lower safely. Before trying an unfamiliar single-pitch route, read the guidebook carefully, ask nearby climbers, and/or research the climb online to be sure it doesn't require a 70-meter rope to descend safely. When in doubt, bring a longer rope or trail a second rope.

Another scenario frequently leading to single-pitch lowering accidents is a climb where the difficulties begin after scrambling five or ten feet to a high starting ledge. The anchors at the top of such routes may be set in such a way that there is plenty of rope to lower the climber back to the ledge, but *not* all the way to the ground. Or the belayer may need to be positioned on the starting ledge in order to have enough rope to lower the climber safely. Again, do your homework, ask other climbers, and always watch the end of the rope as you're lowering a partner.

FIGURE 1: The double-fisherman's knot is an excellent stopper knot for the end of a belay rope or rappel ropes.

If there is any doubt about the length of the rope being adequate to lower a climber safely, tie a bulky stopper knot in the free end so it cannot slip through the belay device. (The double fisherman's knot is a good choice; see Figure 1.) Better yet, the belayer can tie into the free end, thus closing the system.

As you belay a lead climber on a long pitch, keep a close eye out for the middle mark so you're aware of whether there is enough rope to lower the climber. Once the middle of the rope passes through your belay device, you and the climber need to be on high alert. Rope stretch may provide a little extra room for the climber to be safely lowered to the ground, but in such cases the system should always be closed as discussed above. When in doubt, the climber should call for another rope and rappel with two ropes.

As the climber lowers, it's natural to keep an eye on her, but as the belayer you should also be watching the pile of free rope on the ground. Once there is less than 10 or 15 feet remaining, make a contingency plan for safely completing the lower. For example, will the climber have to stop on a ledge and downclimb? Will you need to move closer to the start of the route? Never let the last bit of rope slip through the device if the climber is still lowering, even if she is only a foot or two off the ground—the sudden release of tension can lead to a free fall and tumble.

When lowering in the multi-pitch environment, the belay system must be consciously closed by having the non-load end of the rope tied to the belayer, the anchor, or something else to prevent it from passing through the belay device. In a multi-pitch rappelling scenario we close the system by knotting the ends of the rappel ropes, making it impossible to rappel off the ends.

Miscommunication

The three key problems with communication between climber and belayer are 1) environmental, 2) unclear understanding of command language, and 3) unclear understanding of the intentions of the belayer and climber.

Environmental problems include the climber and belayer being unable to see each other because of the configuration of the route and/or the distance between the two; weather conditions such as wind, snow, or rain; and extraneous noises, such as a river, traffic, or other climbers shouting commands or chatting nearby.

In popular climbing areas with many parties on routes near each other, climbers sometimes mistake a command from a nearby party as coming from their partner. It's always a good practice to use each other's names with key commands: "Off belay, Fred!" or "Take, Jane!" When one climber is at the top of a single-pitch climb and rigging the anchor for a lower-off, top-rope, or rappel, it can sometimes be helpful for the belayer to step back temporarily so he can see his partner at the anchor and improve communication. When the climber is ready to lower, the belayer can move back to the base of the climb to be ideally positioned for the lower.

Especially with a new or unfamiliar partner, it's essential to agree on the terms you'll be using to communicate when one climber reaches the anchor. What do you mean by "take" or "off" or "got me?" Avoid vague language like

"I'm good" or "OK." Agree on simple, clear terms and use them consistently. One common misunderstanding seems to be the result of the similar sounds of "slack" and "take." When top-roping, consider using the traditional term "up rope" instead of "take" for more tension in the rope, as the former won't be confused with "slack."

Before starting up any single-pitch climb, it's critical that belayer and climber each understand what the other person will do when the climber reaches the anchor: Will the climber lower off, and if so what language will she use to communicate with the belayer? Or, will she clip directly to the anchor, go off belay, and rappel down the route? Many accidents have resulted when the belayer assumed the climber was going to rappel instead of lower, or the belayer forgot that the climber planned to lower, or he misunderstood a command ("off" or "safe" or "I'm in direct") as an intention to rappel. Before taking the climber off belay, the belayer *must* be certain that this is the climber's intention. If you have agreed that the climber will rappel, wait for the climber to yell "off belay," and then respond "belay off," and only then remove the rope from your device.

When you reach the anchor at the top of a climb, don't just clip in, shout "take," and lean back. Make sure to hear a response from the belayer indicating that he has you on belay and is ready to lower. If you can't see the belayer, sometimes it is possible to extend your anchor connection or lower yourself a little, holding onto the "up" rope, until you can get into position to make visual contact with the belayer and assure you're still on belay.

A consideration when lowering someone from above is that the belayer and climber become farther apart during the lowering process, and this may compromise communication. To mitigate this potential problem, I like to position myself where I can see, and hopefully hear, the climber being lowered from start to finish. In some terrain this requires extending the anchor's master point.

Belay System Errors

A common cause of lowering accidents is belayer errors, especially when the belayer is inexperienced, inattentive, or unfamiliar with the operation of a particular type of device. Make sure your belayer—or any belayer you observe—knows what he's doing and pays attention until his climber is safely back on the ground or at an anchor. Don't accept or ignore shoddy belaying!

On single-pitch routes, two things that may cause problems are belayers positioned too far back from the base of the climb—and thus getting pulled off balance and possibly losing control when the climber weights the rope—as well as using an unfamiliar device. Switching between tube-style devices, such as an ATC, and assisted-braking devices like the Grigri can cause inexperienced belayers to mishandle the device. Beware of loaning your device to a belayer unless you are confident that he is well-trained in its use.

What is the appropriate lowering brake for lowering your partner? It's one that provides adequate friction to control their descent over very specific terrain. In some alpine terrain situations, the redirected hip belay may be totally sufficient

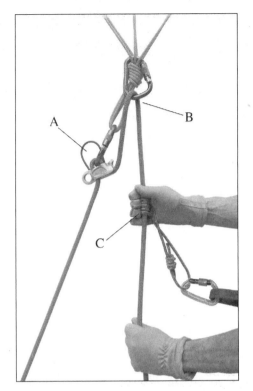 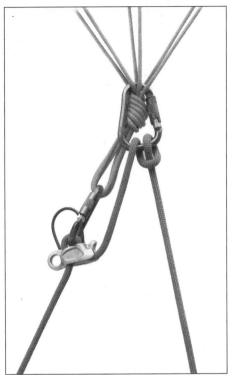

FIGURE 2: Lowering a partner from above with a redirect and backup. A) Belay/ rappel device with locking carabiner clipped to master point. B) Redirect through carabiner clipped to anchor. C) Prusik knot clipped to belay loop as backup—useful for heavier partners or wet or icy ropes.

FIGURE 3: Increasing friction for a lower with a thin-diameter or wet or icy rope, using a Munter hitch on a locking carabiner clipped to the anchor above the belay/rappel device.

for a short, moderate-angle step with high friction. Conversely, lowering directly off an equalized multi-point anchor with a backup may be required in steeper terrain (see Figure 2).

In some cases, the most important belay issue may be anchoring the belayer against a violent upward pull in the event of a leader fall or a falling or lowering top-rope climber who is much heavier. In this situation I like to be tied directly into the climbing rope and use a clove hitch to attach myself to a bottom anchor. This way the length is adjustable so I can be exactly where I want with no slack in the system, and the rope provides shock adsorption if the system becomes loaded.

Most people tend to underestimate how much friction is needed to lower their partner in a safe and controlled manner. How do we gain the experience required to be safe? Through time and practice in varied terrain. Be conservative at first and anchor the belayer, increase friction, use a backup—or all three—

until the belayer has confidence in judging how much friction is needed. It's easy to back up a new climber's belay by holding the brake strand a couple of feet beyond the belayer and feeding the necessary slack. This allows you to closely monitor the belay and provide additional braking if the climber starts going too fast or the belayer starts losing control.

Do you have experience lowering with wet or icy ropes? Do you have experience lowering with modern small-diameter ropes? If not, then I would recommend increasing friction when lowering someone from above (see Figure 3), as well as backing up the lower with a prusik, until you gain adequate experience. Bottom line: If the consequence of losing control of the brake strand is bad, add friction and back it up.

Prior to committing to any lower, consider some "what ifs." For example, what if something happens when I'm lowering my partner and I need to be mobile? How easy is it for me to escape the system? What if I need to transfer this lower to a raise? Does this system allow me to make this transition easily?

Anchoring Issues

There is much to consider when constructing an anchor, but the bottom line is that it absolutely must *not* fail, period. (The Know the Ropes article in the 2012 *Accidents* is a great reference on constructing anchors.) What are some of my concerns when choosing a possible anchor? 1) Will I be using this anchor for climbing and lowering or rappelling? 2) With the resources available, can I construct an adequate anchor in a given spot? 3) How will the rope run once lowering starts? 4) Will the belayer and climber being lowered have visual and/ or audio communication for the duration of the lower?

I have long used the ERNEST acronym as guidance when constructing an anchor. E = Are all pieces in the anchor *equalized* and sharing the load? R= Is there *redundancy* in the anchor, meaning that if one piece fails other pieces will take the load? NE= If one piece does fail and the other pieces take the load, will this be done with *no extension* or shock loading of the remaining anchor? S= Is the anchor material (tree, rock, ice) and/or protection *solid* and *strong*? T= Can this anchor be constructed in a *timely* manner? Just remember, ERNEST should be used as guidance, not a checklist—adjust as necessary.

THE ERNEST ANCHOR

E Equalized
R Redundant
NE No Extension
S Solid and Strong
T Timely

Once an anchor has been established, we must decide how to connect the rope to the anchor.

[This page] Sometimes a route may be too overhanging or traverse too much to clean by rappel. In such cases, it may be necessary to clip into the belay rope while lowering (a.k.a. "tram in") to stay close to the wall and remove each piece. Be sure to communicate each step clearly with your belayer, and never unclip from the belay rope when you are away from the wall (as shown here), because you will plunge straight downward when the tension is released, possibly hitting the ground. Instead, only unclip from the belay rope when you're clipped into a bolt or the belay rope is taut against the cliff face. Make sure to do this in a place where you won't hit a tree or the ground when you swing off. *Andrew Burr*

All top-roping should always be done through the climber's removable gear, such as carabiners attached to quickdraws, runners, or a cordelette, and *not* through the fixed hardware of an existing anchor system. The fixed anchors should only be used for rappelling, where the ropes will be pulled without load. A dirty rope running through the anchor system under load causes unnecessary wear at fixed anchors. In fact, at some sandstone climbing destinations where sand easily works into the weave of the rope, locals are reporting 50 percent wear of steel quick-links in a couple of climbing seasons. So whether you are top-roping or topping out on a sport climb, be responsible and climb or lower on your own removable gear. Whenever possible, the last person to climb should rappel rather than lower off once he is finished with the route.

Before leading a sport climb, decide what extra gear will be needed for the anchor. To set up for lowering and top-roping, I like to carry two quickdraws designated for the anchor, one of them equipped with two locking carabiners. Before following a sport climb, decide what extra gear will be necessary to clean the top anchor. I girth-hitch two 24-inch nylon slings to my harness and add two locking carabiners. When I get to the anchor, I clip a locking carabiner to each rappel ring. Now I can thread the rope through the fixed anchor and rappel. There are a variety of techniques for accomplishing this. Regardless of the one you learn, I recommend practicing while on the ground and using the same system every time you clean the anchor.

One subtle but very important difference between rappelling and lowering is that in rappelling the rappel device is moving over a stationary rope, because the person rappelling is simply sliding down the rope. In lowering, the rope is the object in motion and is moving through a stationary belay device. This means the rope is moving over terrain that may have loose rock and/or sharp edges. In general a taut rope over a sharp edge is not a good idea, and one that is *moving* over sharp edges is just asking for trouble. Before lowering, take extra care to position the rope so it avoids any edges or loose blocks. And, finally, *never* lower with the rope running directly through an anchor sling—the hot friction of nylon on nylon will quickly melt through the sling, with disastrous consequences.

Be Prepared!

As climbers we all need to take ownership in the ability to problem-solve and be self-sufficient at the crag and in the mountains. This starts by critically thinking about what gear we carry on a given objective. For example, I choose to use an assisted-braking device (such as the Petzl Grigri) for top-roping, sport routes, and gym climbing because of the added security and comfort for holding and lowering a climber. In the mountains and on traditionally protected climbs I use an auto-blocking device (such as the Black Diamond ATC Guide or Petzl Reverso) because it is lighter, much more multifunctional, and it allows the rope to slip a bit when catching a fall, helping to reduce impact forces. Another example: I use accessory cord to tie my chalk bag around my waist, so I always have a cord I can easily convert into a prusik if I need to back up a lower or rappel.

In addition to my harness, protection, quickdraws, and shoulder-length slings, here's what I typically carry on most multi-pitch climbs, giving me the tools to deal with most situations that might arise:

- Small knife or multi-tool
- Auto-blocking belay/rappel device with 2 locking carabiners
- 2–3 extra locking carabiners
- 5–7mm* cord to tie on chalk bag, doubling as a prusik cord
- 5–7mm*, 18-foot cordelette with a non-locking carabiner
- Two 48" slings, each with a non-locking carabiner
- 1 extra 5–7mm*, 18-foot cordelette with rappel rings (for multi-pitch alpine routes)
- 24" nylon sling for racking gear

* As a general rule, a cord or cordelette needs to be 2–3mm smaller than the climbing rope in order to provide adequate friction for a prusik.

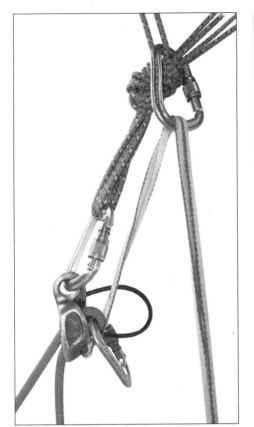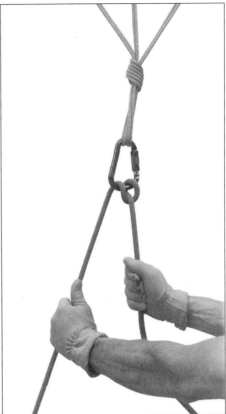

FIGURE 4: When using an auto-blocking belay device in guide mode to belay a second climber, it may be necessary to "release" the locked device when it's under load, in order to lower the second so he can reach a ledge or retry a move. Thread a thin sling through the small hole opposite the clip-in hole on the device, redirect it through the anchor, and clip it to your harness so you can use body weight to release the device. You may redirect the belay rope through the anchor (see FIGURE 2) to gain additional leverage for lowering the climber.

FIGURE 5: The Munter hitch can be used instead of a device to belay or lower a climber. Always orient the hitch so the loaded strand is on the spine side of the carabiner.

Since we are somewhat limited in the amount of gear we carry on a given objective, it makes sense to maximize our understanding of the gear we typically use. One of the most utilitarian pieces of modern equipment is a belay/rappel device with an auto-blocking option, like the BD ATC Guide, Petzl Reverso, or similar. This single piece of equipment has a variety of uses, including the following:

- Standard belay from harness
- Auto-blocking belay from an anchor (see Figure 4)
- Lower from anchor with increasing friction (see Figure 3)
- Lower from anchor with a backup (see Figure 2)
- Simple 3:1 hauling system
- Ascending
- Rappelling

What if you drop your belay/rappel device? A key technique to know is how to tie a Munter hitch and use it to belay, rappel, or lower from a locking carabiner clipped to an equalized anchor (see Figure 5). Remember that the load strand in a Munter hitch must be on the spine side of the carabiner.

All of these skills and techniques should be practiced and perfected at your house, in the climbing gym, or at the local crag, in a setting that has minimal consequences if you get it wrong. And please take the time to read the instruction manuals that come with your equipment. They are packed with invaluable information and tips.

Through time, practice, observation, and reflection we start developing the necessary skills to be a truly competent partner, with the skills to use an alternative system when we, or our partner, can no longer climb, belay, lower, or rappel due to circumstances. I know for certain that we cannot possibly plan for everything that might happen in the mountains, but we all have a responsibility to our partner and the entire climbing community to be as prepared as possible when unexpected situations do arise.

ABOUT THE AUTHOR
Mike Poborsky is an internationally certified rock, alpine, and ski guide, and is vice president of Exum Mountain Guides, based in Jackson, Wyoming.

ACCIDENTS & ANALYSES

LEARN FROM OTHERS' MISTAKES

Charley Shimanski

UNITED STATES

ALASKA

FALL ON ROCK – RAPPEL ANCHOR FAILURE
Denali National Park, Mooses Tooth

On April 20 a party of three Japanese climbers set up a rappel on the route Shaken Not Stirred on the Mooses Tooth. The rappel anchor was a sling around a horn of rock. This anchor failed, resulting in one member of the team, Yudai Sato (24), taking a long fall "head over heels" to the base of the route. His left shoulder was slammed to the ground, but fortunately there was enough fresh snow that there was no serious injury. Suguru Takayanagi (age unknown) was waiting for Sato to complete his descent when he was suddenly dragged off his stance by the climbing rope connecting him and Sato. Takayanagi hit his head on rock as he fell 150 feet to the ground. He suffered a concussion and laceration. He has no memory of the incident, as he lost consciousness when he hit his head.

Two other climbing parties of two each rendered first aid and care for the climber. The rescue that ensued involved two aircraft from the Air National Guard: a UH-60 Blackhawk helicopter and a Lockheed C-130 Hercules. The patient was flown to Anchorage early in the morning on April 21. (Source: Joe Reichert, Mountaineering Ranger, and excerpts from a report by Yudai Sato.)

Analysis

Mr. Sato reported: I believe this accident was caused by the single rock I wrapped the sling around coming loose. I think I should have used two anchor points.

FALL ON SNOW, CLIMBING UNROPED
Denali National Park, Mt. McKinley, West Buttress

Steffen Machulka (49) was a member of the three-person German climbing team "Die Bahner." On May 18 the team was on the eighth day of the expedition and was moving from the 14,200-foot camp to the 17,200-foot camp on the West Buttress. The team climbed unroped up the fixed lines with Machulka in the lead position. National Park Service (NPS) rangers were also moving to the 17,200-foot camp and were close behind.

Around 4:30 p.m., Machulka crested the ridge at 16,200 feet, detached from the top of the fixed line, and set down his climbing pack. According to team member Klaus Dieter, who witnessed the accident, Machulka's climbing pack started to roll down the slope toward the Peters Glacier and he jumped after it. Dieter states that within seconds Machulka was out of sight.

At 4:40 p.m., NPS ranger Kevin Wright arrived at the top of the fixed lines and the accident was reported to him. The National Park contract helicopter 3AE was at base camp conducting training with NPS staff, so Wright requested an aerial reconnaissance of the accident site. Wright and his team began descending the slope toward the Peters Glacier but were unable to locate any sign of Machulka.

At 5:17 p.m., NPS helicopter 3AE launched from base camp to reconnoiter the accident site, with ranger Dave Weber onboard. Shortly after arriving on the scene, they spotted a body at approximately 15,100 feet. The helicopter performed a toe-in hover operation, allowing rangers Weber and Taysom to exit the aircraft and assess Machulka's condition. He showed signs of massive head trauma incompatible with life and was pronounced dead at 5:50 p.m. His body was loaded into the helicopter and transported back to Talkeetna that evening. (Source: Mik Shain, Mountaineering Ranger.)

FALL ON SNOW – SKI MOUNTAINEERING DESCENT, EXCEEDING ABILITIES
Denali National Park, Mt. McKinley, West Rib, Orient Express Couloir

Ilkka Uusitalo (36) and the three other members of expedition "L10 at Denali 2012" left the 14,200-foot camp on the West Buttress route to ascend and then ski down the Orient Express Couloir on May 22. Due to deteriorating weather, the group made an unplanned bivouac on the route and then continued their ascent on May 23. As they were skiing the Orient Express, Uusitalo fell at about the 18,000-foot level in the couloir and slid to approximately 15,850 feet, falling over a rock band in the process. He came to rest about 60 feet deep in a crevasse. His teammates descended to his location and left two members there while one continued descending to the 14,200-foot camp, where he notified NPS rangers of the incident.

Ranger Joe Reichert received the initial notification at 2:30 p.m. Ranger Tucker Chenoweth, who was also at the 14,200-foot camp, and three patrol members were dispatched to the scene. Upon arriving at 3:50 p.m., Chenoweth reported that the other members of L10 had gone into the crevasse and had determined that Uusitalo had died from his injuries. Ranger Chenoweth and his team extracted Uusitalo's body from the crevasse, and it was flown to base camp and eventually Talkeetna, where it was transferred to the medical examiner. (Source: Coley Gentzel, Lead Mountaineering Ranger.)

CARDIAC CONDITION – FAILURE TO INFORM GUIDE SERVICE
Denali National Park, Mt. McKinley, West Buttress

On May 27, Alpine Ascents International (ALP) lead guide Sarah Carpenter of expedition Alp-3-Carpenter arranged to have a 68-year-old client looked after at the 14,200-foot camp by Alaska Mountaineering School lead guide Dan Corn, while the ALP team made a carry to the top of the fixed lines. (It is not an uncommon practice for guided expeditions to assist other guided expeditions on their rest days.) At the time of the arrangement the client was not complaining of any symptoms other than minor fatigue. Later that day, while on a short, guided walk, the client started to complain of extreme fatigue, chest pain, and tingling hands. Corn immediately turned around, took the client back to the 14,200-foot camp, and contacted NPS personnel. They assisted by using a Cascade toboggan to haul the patient the short distance to the NPS ranger camp, where he was assessed by medical personnel.

A detailed medical examination was completed. It revealed that the client had not been forthcoming with information regarding his cardiac medical history with either the ALP admissions team or Carpenter. Rangers determined that his current physical condition and past medical history posed a risk if he were to descend under his own power, and therefore he needed to be evacuated by helicopter. Due to poor weather conditions, he was not evacuated until May 30, during which time he remained in the NPS medical tent, with NPS personnel providing medical care. Guide Carpenter provided his meals and basic needs.

Analysis

The client was aware that he had a serious heart condition. He knowingly kept this critical information from the company and guides who were responsible for his and the expedition's safety. He died of a heart attack a month later, while hiking in Colorado. (Source: Tucker Chenoweth, Mountaineering Ranger.)

(Editor's note: It's unfortunate we have to report this. When individuals do not report known physical ailments, medications being used, or previous injuries, they put themselves, their fellow climbers, and rescue personnel at risk.)

ATYPICAL HACE
Denali National Park, Mt. McKinley, West Buttress

On June 3, an assistant guide (44) with American Alpine Institute radioed to NPS rangers at the 14,200-foot medical camp that he was descending from the fixed lines because he was not feeling well. He arrived at 5 p.m. in the company of Alpine Ascents International guides Don and Sarah Carpenter, who had agreed to bring him down from the top of the fixed lines. The guide's group, led by lead guide Paul Ivaska, continued up to high camp as planned. At the time, the guide seemed unusually tired and unwell, but not seriously ill. While descending with the Carpenters' group, he became increasingly weak, nauseous, and ataxic. The Carpenters carried his pack and assisted him on the fixed lines and on the descent from there to medical camp.

Upon arrival, he was evaluated by NPS volunteer medics Kevin Del Duca and Troy Norman. It was suspected that he was suffering from mild HACE, and a standard regimen of treatment including oxygen and dexamethasone was started. It also appeared that he could have been suffering from severe dehydration and/or heat exhaustion, and he was treated for this as well.

Over the next two days and nights, his condition showed little to no improvement. On June 4, at 1:30 p.m., he was placed into the Gamow bag, and remained in the bag until 2:36 p.m., when he was removed due to inability to tolerate the heat inside the bag. The Gamow treatment produced a slight improvement in the consistent mild to moderate headache he had been suffering throughout the illness, but little to no improvement in his nausea or weakness, and his ataxia remained acute.

On June 4 and 5, medical control was consulted numerous times. Dr. Jennifer Dow could not rule out HACE, but the patient's conservative ascent profile, combined with lack of response to standard HACE treatment, led to suspicion of other neurological problems, including cerebellar infarct (stroke). By June 5, the patient's condition still showed no improvement, and he remained unable to walk more than a few steps without stumbling due to his acute ataxia and extreme fatigue. At this time it was the unanimous opinion among all medical personnel consulted that the patient needed immediate neurological evaluation and hospitalization, and required evacuation from the mountain by air.

The patient was flown to Talkeetna and transferred to a LifeMed helicopter that transported him to Anchorage Providence Hospital for evaluation. He was hospitalized for several days and was eventually diagnosed as having "atypical HACE." (Source: Mark Westman, Climbing Ranger.)

AVALANCHE, WEATHER, POOR POSITION
Denali National Park, Mt. McKinley, West Buttress

On June 12, a four-person rope team triggered an avalanche and was swept a short distance while traveling just below the fixed-lines area on Denali's West Buttress, at the 15,400-foot level. Three of the victims (ages 23, 30, and 32) were members of a University of Alaska Anchorage (UAA)–sponsored medical research study that was investigating the effects and uses of melatonin (the hormone that is supposed to help regulate sleep and wake cycles) at altitude. The majority of the work they were conducting was at the 14,200-foot camp. On June 11, the three climbers joined up with a soloist and traveled up to Denali's high camp at 17,200 feet for a one-night acclimatization trip. The team reported that many climbers had asked to join their team; however, the soloist, who works as some sort of mountain professional/athlete, was invited along due to his expertise.

At 6 p.m., Chris Kerrick notified me via Family Radio Service (FRS) that four climbers had been involved in an avalanche and were OK, but might need medical attention. He and his team had assisted the injured climbers upon their return to camp, but were unsure if their injuries merited immediate medical attention. Approximately 30 minutes later, Kerrick informed me that the climbers were in need of medical care, and he and his assistant guides Eli Potter and Matthew Barela were bringing the injured team to the medical tent.

The chief complaints from each were an injured arm, an injured groin muscle and knee, and two more with injured knees. None of the injuries was life-threatening. Neither were any considered immediately serious by NPS volunteers Kevin Del Duca, M.D., and Troy Norman, R.N. EMT-P. Each patient was treated for the various injuries; two climbers returned to their tent, the third was welcomed into a tent by the "Colombia Epopeya A" team, and the soloist remained in the NPS medical tent, having lost his tent and sleeping bag in the avalanche.

On June 14 the three remaining patients' conditions had not improved. All three displayed difficulty walking; two were unable to walk without assistance.

On occasion, climbers with similar lower-extremity injuries have been able to walk down with assistance from stronger teammates. Given that all team members had been injured, and that none had improved since the time of their accident, ranger Mik Shain at 14,200-foot camp and Talkeetna-based Incident Commander Joe Reichert decided to evacuate three team members using the NPS contract helicopter 3AE.

Being involved in a medical research study, the UAA team had quite a lot of gear with them at the 14,200-foot camp. Teams "Colombia Epopeya," "Taiwan Holistic High School," "Somos Ecuador," and "Bibendum" all assisted in carrying down their gear.

Analysis

The weather conditions and forecast deteriorated significantly during their brief stay at high camp. The four climbers began their descent to 14,200 feet at 3 p.m. Prior to this time, the weather at high camp had been very windy, cold, and snowy, though ranger Mark Westman observed a minor reprieve in the storm from 12 to 1. By 3 p.m., when the climbers departed, the wind and snow had returned, and conditions were reported by Westman to be "very bad."

One of the climbers later reported to me that the team was unaware of how much snow had fallen below them. He also reported that the team noticed signs of instability once they were already on the fixed lines, and that they observed a very small slide immediately prior to the large one that hit their team. (Source: Chris Erickson, Climbing Ranger.)

AVALANCHE – FALL INTO CREVASSE, POOR POSITION, WEATHER
Denali National Park, Mt. McKinley, West Buttress

On June 13, a five-member Japanese expedition, "Miyagi Workers Alpine Federation–MWAF-2012 Denali," was involved in an avalanche while descending the West Buttress of Denali. At an unknown time during the early morning, the expedition triggered an avalanche on a feature immediately above the 11,200-foot camp known as Motorcycle Hill. All five were roped together for crevasse-fall protection, so all were swept into a crevasse.

After an unknown amount of time, survivor Hitoshi Ogi (69) was able to extricate himself from the crevasse. He stated there was no sign of Yoshaki Kato (64), Masako Suda (50), Ms. Michiko Suzuki (56), or Tamao Suzuki (63). Ogi then descended to the 11,200-foot camp.

At noon on June 13, Tim Townsend of expedition "Hard Rock" was packing up camp, intending to descend, when he noticed and took a photo of a new avalanche just above camp on Motorcycle Hill. At 1:45 p.m., while descending from the 11,200-foot camp, Townsend noted a solo climber below him, without snowshoes or gear sled, "weaving erratically between wands, leaving a curvy track that was adding at least 25 percent more distance than a straight line between wands would require." Around 10,000 feet, Townsend's expedition members caught up to the climber, whom they believed was Japanese, and asked if he was "OK." The climber confirmed that he was, and Townsend's expedition continued their descent.

At 4:10 p.m. on June 14, Ogi arrived in base camp and alerted ranger Kevin Wright that there had been an avalanche, and that his other four expedition members were missing. Wright contacted the Talkeetna Ranger Station and alerted them to the situation. Ogi stated that his team was swept by an avalanche into a crevasse, and that the rope they were all tied into had "broken" during the event.

At 5 p.m., helicopter 3AE departed Talkeetna with ranger Dave Weber and myself (Mark Westman) on board. We conducted an initial search and reconnaissance flight over the entire avalanche site. The avalanche was classified as a soft slab avalanche, artificially triggered, with a destructive size of 2 (could bury, injure, or kill a person), and had released within a layer of recent storm snow (SS-A-D2-S). No clues or signs of survivors were found.

On June 15, helicopter 3AE transported rangers Kevin Wright and Mark Westman, along with two volunteers, to the site. A ground search ensued, using avalanche probes, avalanche beacons, and a RECCO locating device. Likely catchment areas and crevasses were identified, probed, and looked into. Avalanche debris boundaries were marked with color-coded wands. At a location mid-slope, just below the presumed trigger point, ranger Wright located gear at the bottom of a crevasse. Descending into the crevasse, Wright found one sled of miscellaneous gear, but no additional clues. At 1:10 p.m., due to deteriorating weather, search efforts were postponed until the next day. Ranger Coley Gentzel and three volunteers (on their way up the mountain) ascended from 7,800-foot camp to the 11,200-foot camp to help with search efforts.

On June 16 we abandoned the search due to dangerous overhead snow and ice hazard, extreme difficulty of extrication, and hazards posed by maneuvering in the confined space. (Source: Mark Westman, Mountaineering Ranger.)

FROSTBITE – EXPOSURE, WEATHER
Denali National Park, Mt. McKinley, West Buttress

On June 13, a guided expedition operated by Rainier Mountaineering Inc. was caught near the summit of Denali in a sudden storm. On the descent to high camp at 17,200 feet, all seven members (ages unknown) of the group sustained varying degrees of frostbite.

The RMI expedition departed the 17,200-foot high camp toward the summit at 12:30 p.m. on June 13. The group had been at high camp for 11 days in mostly poor weather, waiting for a suitable day to make a summit attempt. The group departed in two rope teams. The first team traveled well ahead of the second group, digging avalanche test pits and assessing the snow conditions on the initial section of the slope leading to Denali Pass. As each section was determined safe, the second group would move up to a new location and secure themselves while the lead group continued ahead, making snowpack assessments. At about halfway to the pass, the snow became hardpacked and windblown, and the group moved continuously from there onward. Two guides each reported in later telephone conversations with ranger Mark Westman that at Denali Pass the group had a discussion about the weather conditions and made a decision to continue up toward the summit. One guide reported that the relatively late hour was discussed, and all had noted that the air temperatures were very cold. However, the winds were almost completely calm, there were no high-wind clouds visible, and the group was feeling strong and had been moving at a good pace.

The group continued to the Football Field, where they were overtaken by ranger Westman and Chris Olson, a Volunteers in Parks member, who had left the 17,200-foot camp at 3 p.m. At this time, the group observed snow plumes beginning to stream off the summit ridge above. In addition, vapor banners forming and dissipating overhead signaled the threat of a cloud cap forming over the mountain. One group began to ascend the slope "Pig Hill" with Westman and VIP Olson now in the lead. As the teams approached the crest of the summit ridge at 20,100 feet, the wind, which up to this point had been 15 mph or less, increased to approximately 30–40 mph, and a large lenticular cloud cap formed, rapidly reducing local visibility. This transition occurred very quickly and dramatically, over the span of approximately five to ten minutes.

Around 8 p.m., the 14,200-foot camp recorded a temperature of –8°F, a below-normal reading for mid-June. On this basis, the estimated air temperature at 20,000 feet would be approximately 20 to 25 below zero (F). Westman and Olson reached the crest around the same time this transition occurred. They immediately turned around and began descending for high camp. Throughout their descent, Westman and Olson experienced whiteout conditions and very strong winds, and they each sustained superficial facial frostbite injuries. One team met the descending NPS team about 200 feet below the summit ridge and continued their ascent to the ridge, then along the ridge to the true summit, which one guide later indicated took "less than one hour" from the time Westman and Olson descended past them. The team spent a few minutes on the summit and then began descending.

As they descended the summit ridge, the weather continued to deteriorate and the visibility became very limited. The group reported whiteout conditions between Archdeacon's Tower and the weather station, and were forced to navigate by locating bamboo wands marking the trail. The entire team reported having trouble with iced-up goggles and visibility, and near Denali Pass the guides noticed that one client who had removed her facemask and goggles had sustained frostbite to her face. Once through Denali Pass and onto the "Autobahn" slope, the team became more sheltered from the wind. Near the bottom of the Autobahn, one guide reported that the frostbitten client became very exhausted. One guide remained behind to assist her back to camp at a slower pace, while the remaining members of the group pushed on to camp.

Westman made FRS radio contact with the lead guide at 12:30 a.m. on June 14 as he was beginning to descend the Autobahn. The guide indicated that a few in the team had "minor frostbite" on their faces, but reported no distress or need for assistance. Four of the clients each reported in subsequent phone interviews that frostbite to various fingers and toes in the group was not discovered or confirmed until camp was reached and boots and gloves were removed.

The team descended to 14,200 feet. Two clients were escorted by the lead guide to the NPS medical tent for consultation for their frostbite injuries. One client was diagnosed by volunteer medic Chris Nussbickel as having moderate to severe frostbite extending to all digits on both hands. Another client was diagnosed as having moderate frostbite on all digits of one hand and one digit of the other hand. Two clients and two guides did not visit the NPS camp for medical evaluation, but each of them sustained frostbite ranging in severity from superficial to moderate, in a variety of locations that included the face, fingers, and toes. One client was contacted at 11,200-foot camp later that evening by volunteer medic Kevin Del Duca and volunteer Jason Stiegelmeyer, who noticed that she had substantial facial frostbite, with extensive blistering and swelling that had completely closed her right eye.

The team was flown off the mountain by K2 Aviation on the afternoon of June 15. (Source: Mark Westman, Mountaineering Ranger.)

(Editor's note: Denali can humble the fittest of climbers—including guides. Sometimes people will put the achievement of the summit ahead of physical well-being. It's a matter of choice. In this case, it would be interesting to know what the conversation between the guides and clients might have been.)

HAPE (TWO CASES), APPENDICITIS (ONE CASE)
Denali National Park, Mt. McKinley, West Buttress

On June 16, a guided climber (53) descending from the summit of Denali began experiencing signs and symptoms of HAPE. The climber was able to descend to Denali Pass, at 18,200 feet, but could not travel any further under his own power. The climber's guides from Alpine Ascents International (ALP) were able to successfully lower/pendulum the climber from Denali Pass to approximately 17,400 feet. A National Park Service (NPS) patrol responded to this team's request for help, brought the patient into camp, and rendered medical assistance. No improvement was noted in the patient's condition after 14 hours of medical care, so he was evacuated from the 17,200-foot camp via the NPS contract helicopter.

In a separate incident on June 25, guides from an Alpine Ascents International expedition on the West Buttress contacted rangers at the 14,200-foot camp because one of their clients (53) was experiencing signs and symptoms of altitude illness. Doctor Andy Luks evaluated him at the ranger facility. Dr. Luks believed that the client was suffering from HAPE, and he was treated accordingly. He remained in the care of the NPS until June 29, when his condition and the weather improved enough for his team to walk him down the mountain while he was on supplemental oxygen.

On June 28 an NPS ranger patrol descending from high camp continued to the 11,200-foot camp to assist a guided Mountain Trip expedition with a client (35) who was displaying signs and symptoms of acute appendicitis. After waiting one day for weather to clear in order to evacuate the patient from camp via helicopter, rangers and the two guides escorted him to a location near 10,000 feet, where the weather was better. The patient was flown off from this point with the NPS helicopter and transferred to a LifeMed flight. (Sources: Chris Erickson, Mountaineering Ranger, and Coley Gentzel, Lead Mountaineering

Ranger.)

(Editor's note: AMS, HAPE, and HACE are common occurrences on Denali, the great majority of which are experienced by guided clients. The latter fact is just the luck of the draw, because guides bring their clients to critical altitudes at a reasonable pace. As for appendicitis, it is a bit of bad luck, and not really counted as a climbing accident.)

AVALANCHE
Denali National Park, Mt. McKinley, West Buttress

On July 22, Danish mountaineers Michael Pilegaard (26), Mads Knudsen (30), and Nicolai Bo Silver (26) set out from the 17,200-foot high camp for a summit attempt via a non-standard route up the "Autobahn," the slope leading from high camp to Denali Pass. They had scouted the route variation the previous day, because they were concerned about the high avalanche danger on the standard route. While approaching their intended route up the Autobahn, they triggered an avalanche at approximately 1 p.m. The avalanche swept them from the 17,600-foot elevation several hundred feet down the slope to a point approximately 650 feet from their campsite. Pilegaard, who was relatively uninjured, was able to drag his two companions back to their campsite, where they waited for two days, hoping the injuries would respond to rest and treatment.

On July 25, after determining Knudsen and Bo Silver would not be able to walk, the trio called for assistance on an aviation radio, hoping to make contact with an aircraft providing scenic over-flights of the mountain. A Talkeetna Air Taxi plane heard the call and notified the National Park Service at 11:30 a.m.

NPS set in action a plan to establish two-way communication with the climbers in order to determine the nature and extent of their injuries, location, and other details surrounding their status and situation. This plan also included dropping the team a supply of food, fuel, and equipment, as nothing was known about their available resources.

The NPS contract helicopter was able to deliver the drop bag to high camp, and two-way communication was established between the team and the incident command team in Talkeetna. The NPS staff formulated a plan to carry out an evacuation of all team members starting at 8 the following morning.

The NPS contract helicopter made three successive trips from base camp to high camp and evacuated all three "Hell Tourist" team members to base camp, where they were transferred to waiting LifeMed air ambulances. The uninjured climber was flown back to Talkeetna and provided a detailed account of the events to NPS personnel. (Source: Denali National Park and Preserve News, July 26, 2012, and Coley Gentzel, Lead Mountaineering Ranger.)

(Editor's note: A total of 1,223 attempted to climb Mt. McKinley in 2012, and 498 made it to the summit. The 40.7 percent summit success rate is the second-lowest in the last 25 years.)

ARIZONA

FALL ON ROCK – CAM PULLED OUT, INADEQUATE PROTECTION, NO HELMET, INADEQUATE COMMUNICATION, EXCEEDING ABILITIES
Granite Dells

On January 1 a group of eight college students went rock climbing at the Granite Dells, a climbing area close to the town of Prescott. The rock is composed of granitic formations that resemble the domes of Joshua Tree National Park. The group arrived at the High Rappel Dell, and specifically the "Co-op Area," around 1 p.m. The more experienced members of the group led several single-pitch routes, and all members took turns top-roping the routes.

Sean Hennelly (26) and Cody Brown (20) decided to walk around to the south end of the formation to set up another route. This area is about 200 feet around a corner, and out of view of the group. The wall they decided to climb is about 165 feet tall and historically is climbed in two pitches, due to ledge systems. Initially Sean and Cody were going to set a top-rope on an unnamed broken face and crack climb (5.5) that ended on a ledge about 50 feet up.

Sean was relatively new to climbing, though he had received formal training in traditional anchor placements during an intermediate rock course at Prescott College a few months prior. Sean's instructor described Sean as a "novice leader with a traditional onsight ability in the 5.7 to easy 5.8 range." Cody was relatively new to climbing, with about a year of experience, mainly in institutional settings. Cody had never belayed a lead climber prior to this outing. Sean coached Cody on technique for belaying a lead climber, explaining when to give slack and how to arrest a fall. Once Cody seemed to feel confident, Sean began to lead up to the ledge and a bolted anchor, a pitch he had climbed before. Sean did not have his own rack and decided to lead the pitch on a rack borrowed from a friend who was climbing with the group around the corner. Neither climber was wearing a helmet. The inexperienced belayer was using an ATC-style belay device and was not using a ground anchor.

Cody explained, "The original plan was to set the first pitch as a top-rope from the bolted anchor." Sean placed two pieces of gear within the first 50 feet. When Sean reached the belay ledge, he skipped clipping the bolted belay anchor and continued to climb up and left into what seems to be a variation of the second pitch of Twist Cracks (5.9/5.10). According to his friends, Sean placed a cam about six feet above the bolted anchor.

Sean placed another cam about nine feet above his previous placement, so he was now about 80 feet off the ground, with four pieces of gear placed and with the midway anchor bolts unused. Sean continued upward past his last piece into difficult terrain. Ali Randle, who had just rounded the corner to check on the guys, said Sean seemed to just come off, slightly listing backward, "and then he was in the air." She said her view of the fall was somewhat obscured by trees. Ali said he looked to be in an awkward position prior to the fall. They said he never made a sound while falling.

Sean's highest cam popped when his weight came onto it. He continued to fall onto a very small ledge feet-first, which flipped him upside down. Sean struck the belay ledge below headfirst, less than six feet away from Matt Harry, another climber. The weight of Sean's body came to rest on the next highest cam. He was hanging just off the ledge in an upright position, facing outward and obviously unconscious, about 50 feet off the ground.

Ali, Matt Harry, and Cody all began yelling to the others for help. Greg Malloure and Matt Welsh came from around the corner and scrambled to the ledge to assist Matt Harry. They were able to pull Sean onto the ledge and into a recovery position. Jordan Tidball-Sciullo brought a first-aid kit to the scene and applied a dressing and wet T-shirts to the bleeding area on Sean's head.

Ali called 911 as soon as she got to her phone, which was at the original climbing area around the corner. She tried to speak to the dispatcher, but she was too worked up to speak clearly. Ali handed the phone to Matt Rudnyanszky, who had a difficult time answering the persistent dispatcher's questions. He didn't know the name of the closest road or cross street. He only knew the name of the climbing area. Matt ran down to the highway and located a street sign near the parking area. He told the dispatcher all that he knew.

Captain Ryan Murphy and Engineer Bill Hickey were the on-duty rescue technicians on Prescott Fire Engine 74, along with Paramedic Josh Groves. On arrival they saw the patient on the ledge with Matt Harry, Matt Welsh, Greg and Jordan attending him. Josh Groves said the patient was unconscious and breathing with difficulty, and had a weak, thready pulse. Matt Welsh remained on the ledge and assisted rescuers. CPR and rescue breathing were initiated. Sean was eventually loaded into a litter and lowered to the ground. Paramedics on the ground applied a heart monitor, which showed cardiac activity had stopped. Resuscitation efforts were ceased after a call was made to Medical Control at the base hospital.

Analysis

Have a clear plan. In this case, Cody thought Sean was going to lead up a relatively easy and familiar pitch to set up a top-rope and give Cody a chance to belay a leader. Throughout the climb, witnesses say Sean never spoke. Sean had never climbed this upper pitch before and was unaware of its difficulty. It is unclear why Sean chose to skip clipping the bolted anchor, or why he and Cody never communicated the change of plan.

Know your limits. Sean was onsighting a pitch both unfamiliar and above his leading ability, putting both climber and belayer in a compromising position. Choosing to climb in unfamiliar territory, on questionable gear and with ledge-fall potential, requires an experienced belayer.

Know your gear. Using another person's gear should be a red flag, especially for a new leader, unless you frequently share each other's gear and are familiar with the traits inherent to the brand being used. It could be challenging figuring out SLCD sizes while leading a difficult route.

Wear a helmet. All climbers present that day agree that a helmet might not have saved Sean's life in the event of a life-ending spinal injury. However, it might have given him a better chance of survival.

Know your surroundings and remain calm. The climbers had a cell phone but were unable to give an immediate description of their location to the emergency dispatcher. A member of the group was forced to run to a road and locate a street sign, which took time and delayed emergency crews. Members of the group were unable to talk clearly to emergency dispatchers. Other members of the group as well as rescuers scrambled 50 feet to the ledge unbelayed, which could have created additional patients. (Sources: members of climbing group as listed above; Mike Hennelley; Phil Latham, Prescott College instructor; Prescott Regional Dispatch Center; Captain Ryan Murphy; Engineer Bill Hickey; Firefighter/Paramedic Joshua Groves. Kevin Keith, Prescott Fire Department technical rescue technician, paramedic, and AMGA single pitch instructor, compiled and wrote this report, which was edited by ANAM staff.)

FALL ON ROCK, RAPPEL ERROR
Sycamore Canyon, Paradise Fork

On November 26, while descending to clean a route, Joshua Riggs (22) either fell prior to the descent or hooked up a rappel improperly and fell. Kristin Moore was facing away from the victim and heard an "eek" and his body bouncing off the rocks as he fell.

Analysis

It is possible that Riggs was rigging his ATC rappel device (or re-rigging it) and fell during the process. But in our post-incident investigation, it appears that another scenario is more likely. All apparent indications are that Riggs clipped in to only one line of a two-line rappel system. When Riggs was examined at the bottom of the cliff, his ATC was properly attached to his harness but there was only one rope running though the ATC device. He had been anchored to a juniper tree with a single run of tubular webbing and a water knot. A carabiner was attached to the loop of webbing, and the rappel rope was run through the carabiner, creating a two-rope rappel system. Most of the rappel rope was lying around the body, with the other end of rope lying approximately 20 feet up the cliff.

Riggs had been climbing for three years, mostly on weekends along with several climbing trips where he had done some big walls. Riggs and Moore were now on a climbing vacation and had been at Paradise Forks for two days. They had not climbed the day before because Moore did not feel good about it. On this day, they had previously rappelled off another route and then climbed back up. They had then re-rigged at this location and had rappelled down as before. Riggs had climbed out first so he could belay Moore. Moore said she had not been able to clean all the cams, as they had "over-cammed" near the bottom. After Moore ascended, she was cold and tired, and Riggs told her to lie in the sun while he rapped down and cleaned the route, which is why she was not watching when Riggs begin his rappel. (Source: Edited from a report by Dave Garrison, Coconino County Sheriff's Office.)

CALIFORNIA

FALL ON SNOW, FAILURE TO SELF-ARREST, INADEQUATE EQIPMENT – NO CRAMPONS
Mt. Shasta Wilderness, Avalanche Gulch

On April 21 a man (22) attempted to glissade down Avalanche Gulch below Redbanks. As the snow was too firm, he lost control and slid for 1,500 feet. He suffered abrasions and cuts.

Rangers spoke to the man over the phone and met with him one hour after initial phone contact at a lower elevation. He consented to minor first-aid treatment for cuts and scrapes, and then determined he would continue his self-rescue. He had three or four years of experience. He did not have crampons on. (Source: Nick Meyers, Lead Climbing Ranger and Avalanche Specialist.)

(Editor's note: This is the most common type of accident on Mt. Shasta.)

PARTY SEPARATED, LOST, UNFAMILIAR WITH TERRAIN, EXHAUSTION
Mt. Shasta Wilderness, Avalanche Gulch

On June 16 a middle-aged climber with novice mountaineering skills, Chinyet Lin, was reported missing after an attempted one-day climb up the Avalanche Gulch route. Lin was part of a "meet up" group off the Internet. The party was high on the mountain late in the day when Chinyet decided to take a "nap" at an unknown location. He was out of view of other members of his party, and thus they did not see him along the route on their descent. Chinyet continued toward the top after his nap and summited at 4 p.m. He was not familiar with the mountain and ended up descending the West Face. Fortunately, along the route he met a Shasta Mountain Guides group that aided in his walk back to the trailhead.

Analysis

This is a comment rather than an analysis. We see a number of these "meet up" groups on Mt. Shasta. The first question is, are they pirate guiding? It is a difficult thing to determine sometimes! But more importantly, concerning safety, these groups are people that usually have never met before. We are finding more and more of these climbing parties separating with very little responsibility or care for other members of the group. We think this is because of lack of connection or responsibility, lack of experience climbing together, etc. Basically, it would seem the attitude is, "Let's climb together, but I'm really in this for myself." This is a dangerous attitude. (Source: Nick Meyers, Lead Climbing Ranger and Avalanche Specialist.)

(Editor's note: This was not counted as a climbing accident. It is included because of the "meet up" syndrome. We also call it "Climbing with Blind Dates." Mostly not a good idea.)

COMMUNICATION DEVICE PROBLEM
Mt. Shasta, Hotlum-Wintun Ridge

On August 29 I received a call from Siskiyou County SAR, Celeste Fowler, stating that a SPOT device had been set off on the northeast side of the mountain, near the 10,000-foot level on the Hotlum-Wintun route. The signal came from a commercially guided trip with two guides from Alpine Skills International (ASI).

SPOT devices are set up in this fashion: one button consists of the "SOS" alert; one would push this in the event of an emergency. Other buttons on the SPOT can be assigned personal text messages that the user sets via computer. One can assign any message to the extra buttons.

The ASI team had been assigned one group SPOT device for the trip. However, one of the guides also had a personal SPOT device. On that day, the guide pushed one of the alternative buttons with a pre-determined text message. The message came through as, "We need help, no helicopter necessary, we have enough equipment to stay overnight." This message was relayed to the rangers at approximately 4 p.m. I spoke with both Celeste and Bela Vadasz (owner of ASI), and we all agreed that by the time rangers formulated and got over there and ascended to the party, it would be dark. Since it seemed that the party was "OK," we decided that rangers would head in early the next morning to assist.

Later, just before dusk, Bela left me a message after changing his mind, stating, "Well, if they say they need help, then they need help. Can you go assist now?" Shortly after, another message was received at 9 p.m. from Bela, stating, "Sorry, everything is OK." I did not hear from him again that evening.

I decided that two rangers would proceed with the original plan and head over to Brewer Creek trailhead in the morning, just to be safe. As rangers Coots and Wagenheim arrived at the trailhead at 7:30 a.m., they found no cars. I called Bela to verify that the group had made it out and to figure out what had happened.

Analysis

The guide with the personal SPOT had attempted to change the pre-determined text message assigned to the button just before this trip. He thought he had changed it to, "We are going to be one hour late." Instead, the message was the original assigned text of, "We need help, no helicopter necessary, we have enough equipment to stay overnight." Apparently, he did not successfully change the message, and thus the old message came through. Nothing was wrong with the group, and they had made it out that night.

This was our second SPOT incident of the year. Not much to explain on this one, other than to make sure you change the messages on your SPOT correctly! There is a big difference between, "We need help...." and, "We're going to be one hour late." (Source: Nick Meyers, Lead Climbing Ranger and Avalanche Specialist.)

(Editor's note: This is not considered to be a climbing accident, but it illustrates what can go wrong with the use—or misuse—of such communication devices.)

FURTHER NOTES FROM MT. SHASTA

Mt. Shasta had what most would say was a pretty "normal" season. The spring climbing season was very good, in the way of amazing corn skiing and firm, smooth climbing conditions that lasted into June. Climber numbers were average, with a total of about 5,400 summit passes sold, similar to the last three years. As we moved into summer and fall, there was much anticipation of the 2012 spiritual events that were thought to bring "thousands" more visitors to the area. In hindsight, nothing of note occurred, and the slight increase in day visitors that we saw did not affect climbing numbers on Shasta. On average, the Everitt Memorial Highway leading up the south side sees 100,000 visitors annually.

There were no fatalities and a low number of searches and rescues. In Castle Crags, we had zero incidents. We did have two interesting incidents involving SPOT devices (see one above) and the complications that go along with false/improper activation.

Lastly, I would like to humbly add that while our formal public-assist numbers show only one case, all rangers attest to countless non-formal assists throughout the summer that are not recorded. These can include assisting climbers with very minor injuries and ailments, glissade and descent techniques, ice axe and crampon use, Leave No Trace and wilderness ethics, route finding, gear failure or lack of adequate equipment, winter camping skills, sanitation management, trash, and weather. (Source: Nick Meyers, Lead Climbing Ranger and Avalanche Specialist.)

FALL ON ROCK, RAPPEL ERROR – FAILED TO CLIP TO ANCHOR
Yosemite Valley, Super Slide

On March 24 a man (27) and a woman (26) were rappelling to the base of Super Slide (5.9) at the Royal Arches area. Apparently they wound up between two of the regular rappel anchors. The man built a temporary anchor for the woman to clip into while he ascended to reach the correct anchor. During his absence the woman somehow became unclipped from the anchor (or was never clipped to it) and fell approximately 100 feet down a steep slab to the ground. She survived—in fact she called 911 herself—but her legs were seriously injured, and one was later amputated. Rescue required a basic litter evac to an air ambulance.

Analysis

These were experienced gym climbers, but only had done three years of outdoor climbing. The anchor itself was confirmed to be good when examined later by experienced climber-rangers, so it may have been a mistake in clipping to the anchor or in adjusting the tie-in later. Secondary factors might include descent-route planning and rope management during the rappel. This is a straightforward descent. Inexperience is probably behind all factors. (Source: John Dill, Ranger.)

(*Editor's note: Rappel errors once again are found throughout this edition. Our "Know the Ropes" educational piece from last year needs to find a larger audience.*)

FALL ON ROCK – RAPPEL ERROR
Yosemite Valley, Royal Arches

On May 23 an experienced climber (male, 23) fell while rappelling. He self-rescued and reported the accident when he came to the medical clinic. This is what he wrote on our form: "Rapped off ends of rope on RA descent attempting to clip last bolt station above fourth-class terrain that goes to final rap. Fell 35 feet down slab and impacted with chimney and rock slab. No knots in ends of rope. Possible (likely) talus fracture and ankle sprain. Always tie end-knots and back up rappel." (Source wishes to remain anonymous.)

FALL ON ROCK, PROTECTION PULLED OUT – INADEQUATE PROTECTION
Yosemite Valley, El Capitan, Nose

On May 30, Mike Drake (22) was leading when his top aid piece failed on the upper half of the "Pancake Flake" (pitch 23, 5.10a C1), above the Great Roof. He fell about 25 feet, striking a couple of ledges; he attributes the long fall to having back-cleaned a good piece, thinking he'd need it later. His partner lowered him to the belay and got him into their portaledge. NPS personnel lowered rescuers to him from the summit. They packaged him in a litter, continued lowering with him to the ground, and transferred him to an air ambulance.

He was diagnosed with a fractured elbow, four fractures of the pelvis, four fractured ribs, and a collapsed lung. (Source: From a self-report by Mike Drake on Supertopo.com in October 2012. Search "Falling on the Nose: A Four Month Journey.")

Analysis

Contributing factors included nder-protecting (back-cleaning the piece) and possibly not taking a large enough selection of pro on the pitch. In his excellent trip report at Supertopo, Mike points out the risks of a skimpy rack and of back-cleaning on aid. (Source: Mike Drake via John Dill, NPS Ranger.)

WEATHER – THUNDERSTORM CAUSING FALLING ROCKS, INADEQUATE CLOTHING AND EQUIPMENT – LEFT AT BASE OF CLIMB
Yosemite Valley, Middle Cathedral Rock Descent Gully

On June 4, Joe Ripperger (50) and Claire Epperson (25) climbed the East Buttress (11 pitches, 5.10c). The forecast for the day called for temperatures in the low 80s with a 15 to 30 percent chance of rain, so they started climbing at 6 a.m. They left their warm clothes (fleece) at the base and climbed in T-shirts—because of the warm forecast—but they did carry lightweight rain gear and headlamps. They summited by 2 p.m. with no problems, except for getting off-route for an hour. At 3:30 they started rappelling the descent gully, normally a scramble with short rappels.

Dark clouds had been moving in since about 1 p.m., when they were one or two pitches from the top, but there had been no rain. Claire was 50 to 75 feet down the first rappel on their 60-meter lead line, and Joe was at the top of the gully, when a thunderstorm opened up. Within a couple of minutes a flash flood poured over the top of Middle Cathedral, bringing rocks down with it, one of which dented Claire's helmet. She tried to stem the narrow gully sides but was caught in the flood anyway, with water at thigh level. It was very noisy. They had to communicate by screaming at each other. The rappel line was caught under falling rocks, but Claire was able to prusik about 10 feet and reach the tag line, which Joe had let slide down the lead line. Now he could belay and pull her while she hand-over-handed up the rope. Their lead rope was trapped in the gully, leaving them at the top with only the tag line. Both were now soaked and becoming hypothermic despite rain gear. They spent several hours looking for another way down, knowing it was unlikely. It was now dark, with temps down to 40 to 45 degrees (F) and dropping.

Around 8 p.m. they decided that the gully was their only way out. The rain and flood had finally receded to knee level, and the stuck rope had somehow become unstuck, so they managed to get down by rappelling single strands simultaneously and leaving both ropes behind. By this time they had stopped shivering and no longer felt soaking wet. However, they were unsteady and having trouble concentrating because they were so cold. They got to their car near midnight. They did not go back to the start of the climb for their pack. Joe called us the next day to report the incident so we wouldn't start searching if someone reported the abandoned ropes and clothing.

Analysis

Joe Ripperger has 30 years of climbing experience, including Zodiac on El Cap and other routes in Yosemite, and winter ascents in Canada. Claire has five years of climbing experience. She leads trad 5.8, follows harder, and has climbed in Yosemite and elsewhere with Joe.

They lost an hour or so getting off-route on the climb, but that's common, and you can't always avoid sudden changes in the weather, especially if these changes are very different from the predictions. The lack of warm clothes put them in danger, but they were smart to get an early start and to carry rain gear, tag line, and headlamps. There is plenty of firewood up there that would work even if wet, but they had no fire kit.

They had a personal locator beacon (PLB), but they didn't think anyone would be able to come up the gully that night and didn't think they would survive the night anyway, so they didn't activate it, figuring they had to get out on their own. Their cell phones got no service in the Valley so they had not brought them on the climb.

In Mr. Ripperger's words: "Most of us climb light, with only the gear we'll need for the climb and descent. In the past, I've always gotten away with that strategy. On Middle Cathedral it was different. Although we were prepared for rain on the route, we weren't adequately prepared for a 50°F drop in temp! Especially in summer. So, it wasn't the rain that got us, it was the sudden cold temperature. Now I'm including a fire starter on every climb where there might be access to wood, and an emergency shelter. And I won't be leaving my fleece behind in order to save a little weight. It's remarkable how fast things can crap out and deteriorate. Experience is indeed important, but it doesn't substitute for adequately preparing for a cold overnight. I learned that the hard way."

For a more extreme incident involving these same hazards, see Cathedral Peak, *ANAM 2008*. (Source: John Dill, NPS Ranger.)

FALL ON ROCK, OFF ROUTE
Yosemite Valley, El Capitan, West Face

On June 6, Rick Barus (26) was leading pitch 16 of the West Face, just above Thanksgiving Ledge, when he took the left of two possible cracks. It turned out to be the wrong crack and it petered out. His partner was out of sight below, and they could not communicate against the wind, so instead of lowering he set good protection, climbed a little higher, and tried to traverse to the correct crack about 30 feet to the right. The traverse turned out to be harder than it looked. He kept going, made a dynamic move, and got his fingers in the crack but fell. He took a 25- to 30-foot swinging fall on a fairly clean face; his protection held, but his foot struck something, severely dislocating his ankle. A nearby party called 911, and he was rescued by helicopter short-haul fairly quickly.

Barus' ankle required surgical reduction and hardware. Recovery took six months. His ankle has a slight decrease in range of motion, but he's climbing again.

Analysis

Although this trip to the park was their first time climbing together, Rick and his partner were a compatible team. They had no problems until the accident.

Getting off-route happens. A topo might have helped, but they had lost their only copy. If you find yourself in Rick's predicament, consider downclimbing before traversing, leaving protection above you to lessen the severity of a fall. In a worst-case scenario, downclimb or lower off the entire off-route section, pull the rope through your protection, and start over. In some cases the follower may be able to safely swing over to recover your abandoned gear.

As Jeff Jackson pointed out in a *Rock & Ice* report on the incident, "The West Face and East Buttress are infamous for difficult route finding.... Barus is a self-described 'newbie' with just two seasons of outdoor climbing under his belt. Route finding is a skill that develops over time.... Take some time to study guidebooks, talk to locals, and preview the route with binoculars." (Source: John Dill, Ranger, and *Rock and Ice*, October 2012.)

FALL ON ROCK – RAPPEL ERROR
Yosemite Valley, El Capitan, East Ledges Descent

On June 17, a 51-year-old male French climber was rappelling one of the descent lines on the East Ledges of El Capitan. On the final rappel he fell 30 feet to the ground, injuring his ankle. Details are not clear because of the language barrier, but here is our best guess at what happened, based on a translation of a brief conversation with the subject.

We think he was rappelling with a descent device (type unknown) while carrying a fairly lightweight haul sack on his shoulders. His ropes did not reach the ground, but he was able to reach a fixed line that did. Unfortunately, no stance was available and the wall was steep, so he had to transfer from his original ropes to the fixed line while suspended and weighting either his original rappel device or an autoblock that was tied underneath it.

With the fixed line, he tied a Munter hitch on a carabiner on his harness, transferred his weight to it, disassembled his original rappel rig, and continued down. Somehow the Munter opened the gate of its carabiner and the rope popped out, and he fell the remaining 30 feet to the ground. The haul sack absorbed some of the blow, but he injured his ankle severely enough—a probable fracture—that he had to be rescued by helicopter short-haul.

Analysis

The climber lives in Chamonix where he is, or was, a member of a SAR team for more than 30 years. He did climb El Cap, so we can assume he is experienced.

We are sure he was using the Munter hitch but not sure if it was on the fixed line or on the original ropes; however, the scenario above makes the most sense, and the translation implies that. We don't know if the failure occurred as he was making the transfer or later, while rappelling on the fixed line. We don't know whether the carabiner was a single non-locker, a locker, etc. The point to be made here is that a Munter hitch should always be used with a locking carabiner.

We think the autoblock was on the original rope, below his descent device, and holding his weight. This would have kept his descent device under tension, preventing him from removing the device to rig it on the fixed rope, which would have led him to rig the Munter. That should not have caused the accident, however. More likely is that he depended on a non-locking carabiner for the Munter. (Source: John Dill, NPS Ranger.)

FALL ON ROCK, LOOSE ROCK – ROCKFALL, FAILURE TO TEST HOLD
Yosemite Valley, Sentinel Rock

On June 20 two experienced male climbers (32 and 39) from Japan were scrambling down the gully behind Sentinel Rock (the standard descent), after climbing the Steck-Salathé route (16 pitches, 5.10b). One warned the other of a possible loose slab. The other used it for balance, but it slid on sand, hit him, and sent him on a tumbling fall. His partner went for help. We short-hauled the patient. The fall resulted in a fractured lumbar spine and pneumothorax, but he's making a full recovery. (Source: John Dill, Ranger.)

FALL ON ROCK – INADEQUATE BELAY, LOWERING ERROR
Yosemite Valley, Churchbowl

On July 18 a male leader (20) had climbed Uncle Fanny (one pitch, 5.7) on a 60-meter rope and was being lowered by his partner on the ground, so the rest of the group could top-rope the pitch. The belayer (male, 22) was looking up, helping the descending climber negotiate a ledge. A third member of the group, new to climbing, was standing nearby, as were other parties, and there was a bit of chatting back and forth. Suddenly the end of the rope ran through the belayer's hand and his belay device. The climber fell 10 to 15 feet to the ground, landing hard on his back and striking his head. He doesn't remember the first couple of minutes after the fall, but luckily he missed all the sharp rocks. He had a mild concussion and a minor crack in his pelvis (iliac crest), but he was released and able to walk out of the hospital ER the same day.

Analysis

Another party had just climbed and lowered from the route, so this party figured that only one of their 60-meter ropes would be sufficient, and there was no discussion of tying a stopper knot. Then they forgot to verify their assumption when it counted. It turned out that the previous party had a 70-meter rope, giving them 15 feet to spare. The injured leader normally didn't wear a helmet or knot the end of the rope for top-rope climbs, but he does now, and all members of the party know to keep one eye on the rope. Other climbs at Churchbowl have similar dimensions, resulting in dropped-climber accidents there almost every year. Belayers are intent on watching the leader, and appropriately so, but they may forget about the rope and don't seem to notice the end getting lighter as it rises off the ground. Whether lowering or rappelling, tie that end knot, and if you think that this is just a beginner mistake, see the report for May 23. (Source: John Dill, NPS Ranger.)

FALL ON ROCK – RIGGING ERROR
Yosemite Valley, El Capitan, Salathé Wall

On July 28, Ginnie (32) and Carl (23) were practicing aid climbing on the 165-foot first pitch of the Salathé Wall. They had recently climbed some of the Valley's long 5.11 classics, including Free Blast, the Rostrum, the Regular Northwest Face of Half Dome (in a day), and Astroman, and had decided to spend a few days learning the aid skills needed for big walls. Carl had a little aid experience, but it was completely new to Ginnie. She led the pitch on aid and rigged a hanging belay. While Carl jugged and cleaned the pitch on the fixed lead line, she set up her haul system for the first time, but the haul line somehow became jammed in the pulley before she'd even hauled the bag. They both looked at the mess and the time—it would be dark in an hour—and decided that was enough for the day. They could practice again tomorrow.

Ginnie started breaking down the rigging at her anchor and setting up a rappel while Carl rappelled the lead line. He was cleaning up gear at the base with his back turned to the wall when he heard Ginnie shriek, then a thud. He spun around and saw her lying on the ground next to the haul bag. The bag was covered in blood and she was bleeding from her mouth, but she was conscious and stood up, tearing gear off her harness. Carl, a WFR, tried to stabilize her neck and calm her down. Then he checked her spine and told her to stay still while he called 911. She remained fairly alert, even normal at times, but repeated the same questions over and over, a strong sign of concussion. Her major injuries turned out to be two fractures of the jaw and one of the cheekbone, with nothing life-threatening. She's fully recovered and climbing again.

Analysis

After the fall her ATC was found clipped to her belay loop but not rigged to the ropes. Both ropes were on the ground and tied together as if for a double-rope rappel. A figure-eight loop in the lead line, near where it joined the haul line, was clipped to a reinforced gear loop on her seat harness.

Ginnie remembers securing herself to the anchor bolts with one adjustable daisy and a double-loop figure eight in the lead line, and temporarily securing the lead line to that reinforced gear loop. She remembers untying the leader's end of the rope from her harness as she began to re-rig her system for the rappel to the ground. And she remembers the haul system still holding the haul line. All subsequent events at the anchor are blank, conflicting, or unreliably hazy.

While several scenarios are consistent with the few facts we have, we cannot answer the question that Ginnie asked repeatedly after the fall: "What happened?" One conclusion is clear, however: A very experienced and skilled climber somehow unintentionally disconnected herself completely from her safety system. Ginnie explained later that she was dealing with a new situation and trying to clean up the confusing mess of gear. "There was no failure other than my own mental mistake. I didn't pay attention," she said.

But how did she survive a 160-foot fall to the ground—the equivalent of falling off a 16-story building? Given her proximity to the bloody haul bag, it's possible the bag broke her fall. But her orientation would have to be just right for it to cushion all of her body, and a haul bag is not certified as a 160-foot crash pad. Second, it's possible that the ropes were rigged in a way, or twisted together enough, that unintentional friction slowed her fall and her bodyweight was partly held by that reinforced gear loop. It's even possible that she was partway down a controlled descent when the incident occurred, so that the fall was shorter and her survival less of a miracle. We just don't know.

The take-home points are well-known: New situation or not, expert or not, back up your safeties and keep a constant eye and even a finger at times on the critical elements of your rigging. (Source: Ginnie, Carl, and John Dill, NPS Ranger.)

RAPPEL ERROR, STRANDED – OFF ROUTE, UNABLE TO REASCEND RAPPEL ROPE, INEXPERIENCE
Yosemite Valley, The Nose

On August 4, Richard (18) and Chris (19) attempted to rappel the established Nose rappel route (20+ rappels) from the summit of El Capitan. They felt they weren't ready to climb El Cap, but after seeking advice on Supertopo.com they had decided the rappel was within their capabilities. They got a rope stuck near the top (apparently forgot to remove a knot) and decided to cut it, leaving them two ropes. The correct rappel from Camp V (about a third of the way down) wasn't obvious, so Richard decided to rappel straight down, while the proper line followed the climbing route a short distance to the right. He was unable to reach an anchor and eventually found himself at the lip of the Great Roof.

The normal procedure in this situation is to climb the rope back to the anchor and explore a different direction, but Richard was unable to ascend, possibly due to a combination of inexperience and lack of gear—he'd left his ascenders with Chris at Camp V, although he did have prusiks. Chris offered to descend to help him, but after struggling on his own and getting nowhere, Richard requested a rescue. The NPS tried to coach him up his lines via FRS radio from the Valley floor, but he was weakening, low on water, and helpless. The rangers were worried he might succumb, so the SAR team lowered on ropes from the summit and rescued both of them. (Source: John Dill, NPS Ranger.)

Analysis

Space in *Accidents* does not permit a full description and analysis of this incident. There's a very long thread on Supertopo.com (climbers-forum/1886785/ Rappelling-El-Capitan), starting with Chris asking other climbers for advice prior to the attempt, and including Chris' subsequent account of the incident.

Each member is responsible for assuring the other is skilled and equipped. This may mean doing shorter descents to develop and assess skills before trying El Cap. Just as much could go wrong, but the climbers would be less isolated. (Source: John Dill, NPS Ranger.)

STRANDED – INATTENTION
Yosemite Valley, Cookie Cliff

On December 20, I (Zach, 28) spent the day rope-soloing at Cookie Cliff. As the sun was getting low, I decided to use the rope on Outer Limits to solo Crack-A-Go-Go, a 5.11c crack to the left. I got up the route and clipped my daisies to the anchor bolts. From there the rope angled sharply up and right to the Outer Limits anchor.

On most routes that day I had been belaying with a Mini Traxion clipped to the belay loop on my seat harness. When it came time to descend, I just left the rope in the Mini Traxion and hung from it for security without even clipping the anchors. All of these fixed lines had hung straight down the routes, so there was no risk of swinging sideways. I rigged a rappel with my ATC and clipped it to the belay loop. The two devices sometimes got in the way of each other as I rigged, but it was only a minor hassle.

This time, since the rope angled away from Crack-A-Go-Go and there was no good stance, I faced a big swing and couldn't just hang on the Mini Traxion, so I clipped the anchor for support. Then, to avoid the annoyance of rigging the ATC next to the Mini Traxion, and without thinking through the consequences, I released the rope from the Mini Traxion. In an instant it swung out of reach toward Outer Limits. In the same instant I realized my error and my predicament. The last climbers had left minutes earlier, and it was getting dark. I was dressed in a T-shirt, I'd left my phone, coat, and headlamp on the ground, and the temps were forecast to be mid-20s that night. I started yelling right away, but with no houses around I was dependent on someone driving by 150 yards away with the window open and the radio off! In a way I'm glad that the pitch was so thin and hard, or I might have been tempted to try downclimbing.

I had told my wife I'd be home by 10 p.m. She called the park a little before 11, and a buddy suggested where I might be climbing. The rangers found my car, hiked up to the base, and flipped the rope to me. I'd been shivering for six or seven hours with a full night to go.

Analysis

If I had released a rope earlier that day, it would have remained within reach but alerted me to the risk. By the end of the day, I was so complacent that, as I opened the Mini Traxion, the danger never crossed my mind. In slightly different circumstances—a remote area or stormy weather—such a simple mistake could have been fatal. It's a good thing I had a wife who wanted me back and a buddy who knew where I climbed. (Source: Zach and John Dill, NPS Ranger.)

FALL ON ROCK, INADEQUATE BELAY
Squaw Valley, Big Chief Access Road

On June 9, Eric Johnson (23) of Reno fell approximately 40 feet off one of the area's popular climbing routes, breaking both heels and a vertebra. He fell after his climbing partner failed to secure an adequate belay. (Source: *Sierra Sun*, June 12, 2012.)

(*Editor's note: We include this brief report because it highlights the theme of our "Know the Ropes" section.*)

FALL ON ROCK, CLIMBING ALONE
Matterhorn Peak, Sawtooth Ridge

Early in the morning on Saturday, June 30, Michael Ybarra (45) set out by himself to traverse the Sawtooth Ridge, according to his sister and Alex Few, a friend. He was scheduled to return from his climb by Sunday evening at the latest. After he didn't contact Ms. Few as planned, nor respond to her efforts to call, email, and text him, she contacted local search and rescue personnel on Monday.

Authorities from Mono County and Yosemite National Park conducted a search for Ybarra, including by helicopter. He was located, deceased, on the park side of the ridge, and his body was recovered. He had signed the Matterhorn summit register on June 30 and continued west along the ridge. His rope was found some distance above his body, still coiled. He may have been downclimbing to save rappel gear, but the cause of the accident is unknown.

Ybarra was an experienced climber and had been a journalist with *The Wall Street Journal* and *The Los Angeles Times*, as well as author of a book, *Washington Gone Crazy*. (Source: John Dill, NPS Ranger, and *The Wall Street Journal*, July 5, 2012.)

(Editor's note: To his great credit, Ybarra had told his sister of his intentions. Thus, if he had been injured and not killed, there would have been the possibility that he could have been rescued.)

FALL ON ROCK – ROCK CAME LOOSE
Pinnacles National Monument, Discovery Wall

On April 23, Al Shaver is leading and I (Steve Nechodom) am following on Lost Horizons (5.8). Both of us are in our 50s, with half a life of climbing experience apiece. We have been trad partners for six years. About 3 p.m., I am going to the right across the 30-foot traverse about 80 feet up. I have just cleaned two pieces in the first eight feet. Now 12 feet across, my right hand stretches to a miniature brick hold, feet smearing lichen, then a dainty, long, right-foot stretch. Brick shears off. Penjy onto outstretched right foot. Wish my leg had still been bent; straight right leg fails to damage the cliff. Stopped by pink Tricam in navel-high horizontal, three feet left of belay ledge and 18 feet above me. "ROCK!" comes out of my mouth. Minor bang on right knee, right ankle not right but functional. Wait, curse, and moan. Climb 15 feet to belay. Tie in, sit down, curse and moan. Decide not to lower off into massive poison-oak field.

Rearrange belay for downward pull. Al leads second pitch to tree belay. I sort out how to leave the belay ledge without stressing right ankle too much, climb 25 feet or so up open book. Switch to hand traverse on the outside of arête. Another half brick blows off from under right foot: no fall, but a solid slam. I yell "Rock!" again. Right ankle yells fat obscenities at me. Stop, curse, and moan. I spend 30 minutes climbing the last 30 feet, and announce the end of the climbing day.

I hobble 20 yards with Al's help to a grassy slope and park my butt while Al goes down to get tape, boots, and food. Eat, tape ankle tightly, and install boot laced really tight. Leave the top of Discovery Wall at 6 p.m., walking sideways so ankle won't bend. Stop every 50 to 100 feet, loosen boot every other stop. Arrive at Al's car at 8:30 p.m., perhaps a half mile, certainly a record for slow. Al drives back to my car in Salinas. I drive with my left foot back to Berkeley. Neighbor unloads my car. Done moving at 1 a.m.

Small crack in talus bone. Transverse tarsal joint pounded to putty, minimal swelling. Five weeks of crutches and air cast. Four more weeks with air cast. Six months later, still using ankle braces.

Analysis

We had done this climb a few months before, and I am sure I used the same half-brick hold on the traverse the first time. The unsure mossy footing caused me to hang harder on the hold this time, and it broke. Pinnacles is known for chossy climbs and rockfall. I am not going to burn my guidebook, just climb with greater care. (Source: Steve Nechodom.)

(Editor's note: "Chossy" is a term that Brits use for climbs that have lichen, moss, wet surface, loose bits, or all of the above.)

FALL ON ROCK – TRIPPED OVER FIXED LINE
San Jacinto Wilderness, Idyllwild, Suicide Rock

On July 24, Karen Gose (27) died of injuries sustained while demonstrating climbing and rappelling techniques on the face of Suicide Rock. Gose, a counselor with a Girl Scout troop, fell 30 feet onto a rock ledge during a rappelling demonstration. CAL FIRE/Riverside County Fire Department responded and lowered a medic to the rock ledge. He attended to the woman and prepared her for a helicopter hoist. She complained of difficulty breathing and was thought to have a broken hip and possible rib damage. At 2:50 p.m. she was hoisted into the helicopter. At 3:04 p.m., attending personnel transferred Gose into a Mercy Air helicopter for transport to Desert Regional Medical Center in Palm Springs. She died en route.

Analysis

Along the base of the Weeping Wall, a ledge runs from left to the right and curves upward toward the base of the left-facing dihedral forming the right side of the Weeping Wall. Gose apparently had a fixed line along this ledge. As one moves leftward along this ledge (toward Bye Gully), the drop-off below gradually increases, though never more than about 30 feet. She apparently had rappelled from the Surprise anchors to this ledge, and as she was unclipping from the rope she tripped over the fixed line, going over the drop-off below.

Not a rappel rigging failure, nor an anchor failure. Simply a very tragic accident. (Source: Edited by Beth Shilliday from a report on Supertopo.com.)

FALL ON ROCK, INADEQUATE PROTECTION
Joshua Tree National Park, Intersection Rock

In October I was leading the Left Ski Track (5.11a) on Intersection Rock and suffered a ground fall from about 20 feet up. I landed in a patch of dirt that is about two feet by three feet. All around the spot where I landed are sharp rocks that could have seriously injured me.

I climbed up past the "fin" area of the climb, which is about 18 feet off the ground, or so it appears. I placed a No. 4 C4 cam behind the flake/fin down low in the pod, clipped the piece, and continued up the climb. I messed up the sequence through the crux and decided to take what I thought would be a short fall to my last piece and start the sequence over again. I told my partner, "Falling," let go, and fell to the ground. My No. 4 cam popped out of its placement, as did a crappy No. 2 below it. I knew the No. 2 was no good, and knew that once my No. 4 had popped, I was going to the ground. I landed on my butt, which broke my fall wonderfully. My arms also broke a bit of the fall, although I didn't hit them hard on the rocks. I didn't hit my spine or head on the rocks at all, which is probably why I ended up in reasonable condition.

After the fall I stayed on the ground for a minute and felt out my injuries. My chest and butt hurt, but other than that I didn't feel horrible. I then stood up and immediately felt pain in my rib cage. As I stood up, I felt some movement in my chest, which was pretty freaky.

My partner took me to Hi-Desert Medical Center in Joshua Tree, where the staff put me through a CT scan. The doctor came in about two hours after the scan and told me that I didn't have any broken ribs, my spine was intact, and I didn't have any organ damage. He said I had soft-tissue damage and cartilage damage at my [costochondral junction], and that it would most likely take a few weeks to heal.

Analysis

Causes of the piece of protection failing: I went back to the site on Sunday and looked at the area where I had placed the cam. The crack is slightly flaring, but not horribly. I have to assume that as I moved past my No. 4 placement, the cam rotated or slid up the crack into a more flaring section. When I fell, the outward pull on the piece popped the cam outward and through the more flaring area of the pod. If I had slung the piece, the piece probably would have not rotated or moved, and it would have held my fall. A better No. 5 placement was available higher in the pod and deeper in the rock. This alternative placement would have been much safer, but I didn't have a cam of this size with me. I have since bought one for such cases.

Slinging pieces that are critical on lead to protect the leader from a ground fall is always a good idea, especially if movement of that piece can jeopardize its integrity. A common complacency error among climbers is to assume that larger protection does not require as much care while placing the piece. I can now testify that larger protection needs just as much care as placing smaller protection pieces.

It was definitely psychological pro. I was not relying on it at all. I knew the next piece I was going to place, which hand I was going to use, and racked it in the appropriate place on my harness. I took an educated risk in relying on that protection and executed everything as planned. I just should have slung the piece.

I also agree with the recommendation of downclimbing and "taking" on the pro if the option is available. I was so confident in the placement that I just took the fall instead. If I had downclimbed, I would have seen that the piece had walked and would have been able to correct it.

I am not proud of this ground fall. It is an embarrassing blemish on my otherwise excellent climbing record. I hope others can learn from my mistake. (Source: Nelson Day, edited from a post on Supertopo.com.)

FALL ON ROCK, INADEQUATE PROTECTION, INADEQUATE KNOWLEDGE OF ROUTE RATING
Joshua Tree National Park, The Cyclops

On November 7, Bob (62) and I (67) arrived in Joshua Tree in celebration of Bob's retirement. We spent the morning top-roping Hands Off (5.8) and practicing self-rescue techniques. Bob said there was a 5.3 on Cyclops Rock, a good first lead for the week. I usually follow but have led for three years, while Bob had led for over 30 years. The fissure called the Eye was directly above the route, and Bob explained that you go through it to descend. We scrambled up a ramp to the base and recognized our planned route wasn't a 5.3—we were actually below Fractured Fissure (5.10d).

Instead of downclimbing, we searched for an easier ascent and found Leader's Fright (5.8), but didn't realize it was R-rated. I planned to set the first three pieces five feet apart. The first piece was bomber, the second at seven feet was tenuous in a shallow crack, and the third at six feet was also tenuous. Next thing I remember, I was lying on my back and staring at the sky with Bob's hands on my chest. The top two pieces had popped. I became unconscious two times and have no memory of the fall or why I peeled off. Bob got the attention of another climbing party for assistance and set up an anchor and lowering rig. The other party failed to return to render assistance, so Bob lowered me, and I was able to walk out. I was driven to the emergency room, and after a CT scan and X-rays, I was released.

Analysis

I would not have led this route if I knew of the R rating because of tricky placements. (Source: Arnold Robson.)

COLORADO

FALL ON ICE, FOLLOWED BY CARDIAC ARREST
Telluride, Bridal Veil Falls

Midday on January 15, Jack Roberts (58), a renowned ice climber and alpinist, died on the 400-foot Bridal Veil Falls (WI5). Jack was leading the second pitch, a long, steep pillar on the right side of the falls, when he fell 60 feet, breaking his hip. His belayer was able to signal hikers below, who summoned the San Miguel County Search and Rescue group. While waiting for rescue, Jack suffered a cardiac arrest and died. Forty minutes of CPR were unable to resuscitate him.

Analysis

According to local climbers, Bridal Veil had been in difficult condition, with a roof on the first pitch and a very steep pillar on the second pitch, where Roberts fell. The second pitch was reportedly wet. (Source: Rockandice.com, January 16, 2012.)

(*Editor's note: Roberts' partner, Jonathan Miller, wrote a full account from his point of view, published at coldthistle.blogspot.com.*)

RAPPEL ERROR – FALL ON ICE
Estes Park, Big Thompson Canyon

On February 18 a female ice climber (49) fell while rappelling during a guided ice climb with her husband and daughter. She was approximately 20 to 30 feet above the ground when she slipped and swung sideways into a protruding ice formation. She was taken to McKee Medical Center and treated for blunt-force trauma to her hip and lower back. (Source: edited from Denverpost.com by Aram Attarian.)

Analysis

We were not able to determine if the guide was belaying her. A good belay might have prevented this incident.

FALL ON ROCK, UNTIED FROM ROPE, LACK OF COMMUNICATION
Boulder, Second Flatiron

Late in the day on January 15, a male lead climber was attempting to climb the Second Flatiron, a low 5th-class climb with many possible variations. The leader climbed a full rope length and could not find an adequate anchor. He untied from the rope to try to climb further to find viable anchors. The second started climbing, assuming he was on belay, and then slipped, fell, and tumbled 40 feet, getting airborne in the process. Rescue involved 800 feet of high-angle evacuation to a ground team, followed by a mile of lower-angle evacuation to an ambulance.

Analysis

It seems as though a lack of experience and available protection led the lead climber to believe the best option for the completion of their climb was to untie and begin a free solo to find suitable anchors. It seems there was a lack of communication between the leader and second, both for the action of untying from the rope, and for the second starting to climb. (Source: Daniel Lack, Rocky Mountain Rescue Group.)

FALLING ROCK – PULLED ROCK OFF, FAILED TO INSPECT TOP OF BOULDER PROBLEM
Flagstaff Mountain

During the early afternoon on May 3, calls for help were reported near Realization Point on Flagstaff Mountain. Rocky Mountain Rescue Group (RMRG), AMR Ambulance, City of Boulder Open Space and Mountain Parks, Boulder City Fire Department, and the Boulder County Sheriff's Office responded to the scene. Bystanders at the trailhead pointed in the general direction of the cries, and responders quickly located a stuck and injured climber, pinned underneath a large boulder, a short distance north of Flagstaff Road.

Andrew Chapman (27) and his girlfriend had been bouldering with a companion on a 10- to 12-foot-tall boulder, and unexpectedly pulled off a large piece of rock (the size of a large boulder). The climber fell backward to the ground and came to rest in a sitting position, pinned against a tree, with one leg pinned between the detached piece of the boulder and another rock. He sustained injuries but was able to breathe normally. He could not extract himself.

Upon arrival, rescuers quickly began formulating plans to move the boulder and free the injured climber. The multi-agency crew completed extrication at

2:47 p.m. RMRG then performed a short scree evacuation to carry Chapman to a waiting ambulance for transport to Boulder Community Hospital. He is expected to make a full recovery.

Analysis

Approximately one percent of climbing accidents RMRG responds to are caused by rockfall. Most of these accidents occur February through June. Seasonal risk increase is presumably associated with seasonal precipitation, freeze-thaw cycles, and climbing use patterns. The first climbers of the season are more likely to pull off loosened rock than the last climbers of the season.

The injured climber remarked that if he had inspected of the top of the boulder problem prior to attempting to climb it, he likely would have noticed the loose rock hazard and avoided it. This accident occurred in a relatively low climbing-use area. In more popular areas, other climbers are likely to have already released loose rock. Climbers are well advised to be particularly alert to potential rockfall hazards from February through June. Added caution is appropriate on less-traveled rock formations or routes. (Sources: Rockymountainrescue.org and Dailycamara.org.)

FALL ON ROCK
Boulder, First Flatiron

On July 10 an inexperienced climber seconding the First Flatiron injured his ankle while being belayed and could not move. The leader did not have sufficient equipment to effect self-rescue. Rescuers climbed to both the injured climber and belayer and rappelled to the ground. (Source: Daniel Lack, RMRG.)

Analysis

Because of the Flatirons' proximity to Boulder and the road, there are frequent incidents of this type. While in many of these incidents the individuals are not really climbers, we have no choice but to count them. (Source: Aram Attarian.)

FALL ON ROCK, BELAY DEVICE COMPROMISED
Eldorado Canyon State Park, Redgarden Wall

On March 31 a male climber had led the fourth pitch of Rewritten (5.7) and was belaying his male partner up the pitch. The second was only about 10 feet from the top of the pitch when he slipped and fell. The lead climber lost control of his belay device (Trango Cinch), and his partner fell as far as 90 feet before the lead climber was able to stop the second's fall. The lead climber suffered rope burns to both hands. The second sustained a sprained ankle and contusions from hitting the rock. Two nearby climbers helped the two injured climbers get to the ground. They walked out and drove themselves to an urgent-care facility, where they were treated and released.

Analysis

It is likely that either the Cinch was loaded incorrectly or the configuration of the leader's belay setup (possibly in combination with being pulled into the rock) prevented the Cinch from moving into a locked position. (Source: Steve Muehlhauser, Park Ranger, Eldorado Canyon State Park.)

FALL ON ROCK, OFF ROUTE, PLACED NO OR INADEQUATE PROTECTION
Eldorado Canyon State Park, Redgarden Wall

On May 24, Adam Kimmerly (32) and William Olszewski (51) set out to climb the Grand Giraffe (six pitches, 5.9+) on Redgarden Wall. William explains: We climbed the west face of Lower Ramp (5.2) to access Grand Giraffe Ledge and the start of our route. Adam led the first two pitches of Grand Giraffe, with me following. I led pitch three and brought him up to my anchor.

Adam was set to lead pitch four, the crux, a consistently wide crack that pulls over a bulge and finishes on Redgarden's Upper Ramp. The guidebook (*Eldorado Canyon*, Steve Levin, Sharp End Publishing, 2009) calls for a standard rack to 3.5 inches for this route, and mentions that 5- to 6-inch gear is optional. We had nothing larger than a 4-inch piece. Adam started up the pitch, and at some point he determined that it was not wise to continue up the wide crack without larger gear and backed off to the anchor.

We remembered that the guidebook also identified a pitch-four variation rated at 5.6 PG-13 that links up with Super Slab. Adam began leading that variation and disappeared from sight to climber's left, past an arête. Verbal communication was lost due to wind and the configuration of the rock. After a few minutes the rope went temporarily slack and then quickly tightened, signaling that Adam had fallen. From this position we had partial verbal communication, and I followed his instructions to lower him back to my anchor ledge. Adam is a SAR volunteer in San Diego County and self-diagnosed a fractured leg.

After securing Adam to the anchor, I called 911 on my cell and was connected to Rocky Mountain Rescue. I handed the phone to Adam, as he has much more experience in such matters. I set a rap anchor, transferred our PAS tethers to the new anchor (utilizing a nut, four-foot sling, two carabiners, and an existing piton) and cleaned my initial gear anchor. We self-rescued to Grand Giraffe Ledge: Adam rappelled to an intermediate ledge with an anchor, then I rappelled; I clipped a carabiner to an existing sling and cordelette that were slung around a large boulder and fixed my 70-meter rope to it, as we were not sure of the distance to Grand Giraffe Ledge. Adam rappelled to the ledge. Upon realizing that the ledge was no farther than one-half the length of the rope, I reset the rope and rappelled to join Adam. By this time members of RMRG were on the ledge, attending to Adam.

RMRG applied a vacuum splint to Adam's right leg and used an assisted lower to get him down to the ground. From there he was placed on a litter and carried down to and across South Boulder Creek. I drove Adam to a local hospital, where X-rays showed multiple compression fractures of the right tibia and fibula. He also had a bruised left heel and sprained left ankle.

Analysis

What follows are the contributing factors to this accident, as I see them:

We had insufficient gear for the crux pitch. While I do not hold the guidebook author or the publisher accountable in any way, we were under the impression that listing the larger gear as "optional" meant that the crux pitch could be led safely without such gear. In fact, that may be possible; however, Adam, an experienced climber, made the determination that it could not be led safely with the gear we had. This led him to opt for the pitch 4 variation instead of continuing up the route.

The fact that said variation was listed as having a difficulty rating of 5.6 gave us the impression that pitch 4 could be circumvented with easy climbing. In retrospect, while the traverse from Grand Giraffe to the third anchor on Super Slab was indeed 5.6, this variation still requires climbing through the Super Slab crux at 5.10d, with sparse protection. While Adam is an accomplished and experienced climber, regularly redpointing slab routes at 5.11, falls are always a possibility, especially near the top of one's abilities.

The crux of Super Slab requires micro-protection, of which we had very little, and most likely insufficient for the task. While the first ascent of this route utilized fixed protection for the crux in the form of hammered pitons, these pitons are long gone and have not been replaced with modern fixed protection, requiring climbers to use micro-protection that may not hold a lead fall.

Conclusion: Had we better researched this route and therefore understood that our options for pitch 4 were a wide crack requiring bigger gear or a difficult slab requiring suspect micro-gear, we would have chosen to climb something else. Had we at least understood that the pitch 4 variation to link up with Super Slab would require a difficult-to-protect 5.10d crux, we would have bailed without attempting the variation. Had the missing pitons at the crux of Super Slab been replaced with modern fixed protection, Adam's lead fall would have been minor, keeping him far away from the sloping ledge that caused his injuries. The bottom line is that a lack of knowledge of the routes, combined with a willingness to go for it and a little dumb luck, resulted in a big fall with serious injuries. (Source: William Olszewski.)

(*Editors note: The climbing party called 911 and provided precise details of their location, injuries, and plans, allowing faster rescuer access and prioritization of rescue and medical equipment. The ability to self-rescue expedited their rescue and is a fundamental skill all climbers should possess.*)

FALL ON ROCK, INADEQUATE BELAY – ROPE RAN THROUGH BELAY DEVICE, NO KNOT IN ROPE-END, INEXPERIENCE
Boulder Canyon, Happy Hour Crag

During the early afternoon on March 24, Ira Lewis (33) climbed Malign (5.7), a one-pitch trad route on the Happy Hour Crag. After Lewis completed the climb, his partner on the ground began to lower him on their 60-meter rope. The belayer was not tied into the rope, and the end of the rope did not have a stopper knot tied in it. When the end of the rope was reached, it pulled through the belay device, causing Lewis to fall 15 to 20 feet.

Other climbers in the area heard the fall, and one hurried down to his vehicle and drove into Boulder to call 911 while others remained with Lewis. Personnel from the Sugarloaf Fire Department, Rocky Mountain Rescue Group, and the Boulder County Sheriff's Office responded, as well as an American Medical Response ambulance.

Both climbers were wearing helmets. Lewis was briefly knocked unconscious and suffered other injuries. He was stabilized by medical personnel, placed into a rescue litter, and transported to the Boulder Community Hospital with non-life-threatening injuries.

Analysis

The belayer did not have basic belayer training to watch for the middle mark on the rope or tie a knot in the end. The leader and belayer did not talk about rope length versus climb distance before beginning the climb. (Source: Boulder County Sheriff's Office, www.bouldersheriff.org, and RMRG.)

FALL ON ROCK – FALL FROM CLIFFTOP, POOR POSITION
Boulder Canyon

On July 11 a climber had just untied from the rope after completing a climb. The climber stepped backward at the belay area and fell over a small cliff. (Source: Daniel Lack, RMRG.)

Analysis

Over the years, we have seen a number of these incidents. Letting down one's guard after the climb and not being anchored, especially when in an exposed position, create the potential for a fall. Most of these incidents happen at the top of ice climbs. (Source: Aram Attarian.)

FALL ON ROCK, NOT SECURED TO CLIFFTOP
Boulder Canyon, Boulderado

On September 2, Treff Owen Carpenter (28) fell 70 feet to his death while setting up a top-rope climb on the Boulderado crag, located in Boulder Canyon. He was a member of a climbing group of eight, and the most experienced climber in the group. He volunteered to hike to the top of the route to set up an anchor to help an off-route climber. While searching for an anchor, he fell to the ground and was fatally injured.

Treff came to rest on the road, where others secured the scene and administered basic first aid until a nurse and EMT arrived from nearby. Nederland EMTs were on scene within 10 minutes, but were not able to keep him alive. (Source: Daniel Lack, RMRG.)

Analysis

According to Mountainproject.com, "This southwest-facing wall is a [common] place to take a first-time climber. The staging area and the anchor access make it a potentially hazardous climbing location for the unwary climber. It has a number of easy climbs in close proximity up a clean open wall. Anchor placements are a little tricky, though; the ledge up top, while safe, does not afford many things to set up an anchor with. Recommend bringing some long slings and some cams to do the job right. Top-rope access is via a trail up the talus just left of the rock. Be extremely careful accessing the anchors above these climbs if you top-rope here. Lethal accidents have occurred too often here."

FALL ON ROCK, CLIMBING UNROPED, ROCK BREAKS
Clear Creek Canyon, Cat Slab

On May 25, T.J. Brumme (25) was photographing friends climbing in the Cat Slab area of Clear Creek Canyon. He soloed up the far right section of Cat Slab and clipped into the second bolt on a route to take photos. Once finished, he unclipped and then started to downclimb the route. According to friends, the rock he was standing on broke away, causing him to fall approximately 10 feet. During the fall he struck a ledge, knocking him unconscious. He tumbled another 20 feet before it was all over. Brumme escaped with a concussion, a few facial lacerations, and a bruised foot.

Analysis

This accident will definitely make me think twice about soloing anything, no matter the grade. When the rock you're standing on crumbles, there's not much you can do about it. (Source: T.J. Brumme.)

SLIP ON ROCK, PROTECTION PULLED OUT
Front Range, Mt. Bancroft

On September 7 three climbers, Sterling Roop, Adam Pérou Hermans, and Alexander Lee, left Boulder around 6 a.m., planning to climb the mostly fourth-class Direct East Ridge (II 5.4) of Mt. Bancroft (13,250 feet) in the James Peak Wilderness Area.

According to Hermans, "The day was overcast and we had a few big gusts and short bursts of hail, but nothing too rough. The [technical portion of the] climb was not on the main route, but it was easy. Sterling climbed the face with no problem, but walking along the top ledge he slipped, as if on a banana peel or black ice. To our horror his slip propelled him off the ledge, and he rag-dolled back down the face he'd just climbed, smashing and crashing into ledges and the rock wall along the way. At one point a nut placement pulled, causing Sterling to fall further. Fortunately, Alex (on belay) was able hold the fall, and Sterling stopped about eight feet above the ground."

Sterling was upside down, unconscious, bleeding profusely from the head, and making terrible noises. His mouth was full of a foamy, gray liquid. Hermans and Lee called 911 and tended to Sterling as they waited for help to arrive. Hermans continued, "At some points he would try to move, at which point I would need to wrestle to keep him pinned down, as I was afraid of a neck injury and paralysis, and him either sending himself or both of us down the cliff; at this point we were anchored to a steep slope above a perhaps 1,000-foot drop to the valley below." Sterling's alertness and orientation slowly improved, but he still didn't remember what had happened.

Rescuers were first airlifted by Flight for Life to a landing zone close to the accident scene at Lake Caroline, but still needed to climb nearly 600 feet up steep, fourth-class terrain to reach Sterling on the East Ridge. Upon reaching the victim, rescuers began the process of getting an IV in and putting him into a sleeping bag and onto a litter. Because of the location and extent of Sterling's injuries, ground rescuers determined that the safest and fastest way to get him off the mountain was to hoist him via helicopter.

Rescuers were able to haul Sterling to the ridge using an improvised 3:1 mechanical-advantage system. He was then belayed a hundred feet along the top of a narrow, exposed ridge to a small ledge to wait the arrival of the helicopter. Upon arrival, the UH-60 Black Hawk crew assessed the situation to ensure the team could safely attempt a live hoist. The litter was hoisted and then secured into the helicopter. Sterling was transferred to a Flight for Life helicopter that took him to a local hospital. He was released the following morning and was back in the mountains a few weeks later.

Analysis

The climbers noted the importance of remaining analytical when assessing risk. "Even though there was very low risk (in the climb), there was still very high consequence. Accidents can happen when you're in the mountains, even when you're making good decisions. We felt prepared. We felt we had the right experience and the right gear. Risk is always there." (Source: Edited from a news report written by Master Sgt. C.D. Theiral, Colorado Air National Guard.)

FALL ON ROCK, LOOSE ROCK
Maroon Bells, North Maroon Peak

On September 17, Derek Kelley (34) fell more than 600 feet to his death while climbing North Maroon Peak (14,014 feet). According to reports, Kelley was about 300 feet from the summit when he fell after a boulder came loose. Rescue personnel believe he had been wearing a helmet.

Analysis

While it is understood that rockfall and loose rock are common objective hazards in the mountains, it should be noted that the Maroon Bells (a.k.a. "the Deadly Bells") are particularly known for these hazards. (Source: Jed Williamson.)

IDAHO

FALL ON ROCK, INADEQUATE BELAY
City of Rocks National Reserve

At 2:50 p.m. on July 7, climbing ranger Brad Shilling was flagged down by a park visitor who reported there had been a climbing accident and that the climber had a head injury. The visitor pointed to the descent route from the climb Intruding Dike (5.7) on the Breadloaves, about 30 meters from the road. Shilling found Julia Batten (51) lying on her side at the base of the climb. Primary survey disclosed a raised lump about two inches in diameter at the right base of her head. Batten was very disoriented, but during the assessment she complained of pain in her ankles, her right scapula, and her neck. She had distinct retrograde amnesia, and would repeat questions and statements over and over in a one- to two-minute cycle.

Shilling radioed headquarters and requested both a ground and air ambulance to be dispatched to the Breadloaves designated landing zone. A cervical collar was applied, along with a backboard and a splint on both ankles. Oxygen was administered, and the patient was moved to the LZ. Life Flight helicopter arrived at 3:44 p.m. and assumed care of the patient. They lifted off at 4 p.m., bound for Utah.

Batten was taken to the Huntsman Center in Salt Lake City, where she works as a nurse. She was diagnosed with a fractured spine, a concussion, two broken ribs, and a fractured ankle.

Analysis

Batten and her partner, Tosh Lahey, had just finished the Intruding Dike, and Lahey had belayed Batten almost all the way down the descent. Batten requested to be taken off belay before she reached the bottom, and was attempting to climb down the last 20-foot section unroped when she fell. Though the distance of the fall was not far, the landing was among rugged boulders. If she had stayed on belay until reaching level ground, this accident would not have occurred. (Source: Brad Shilling, Climbing Ranger.)

KENTUCKY

FALL ON ROCK, NOT ATTACHED TO BELAY ANCHORS
Red River Gorge, Muir Valley

On March 19 a man (27) was standing on a belay ledge at the Sunnyside Wall when he stepped back too far and fell off the ledge. He impacted the ground about 15 feet below and sustained a back injury. Muir Valley Rescue responded and litter-carried the victim to an ambulance waiting on the Muir Emergency Road.

Analysis

The belayer should have tethered himself to the belay anchors to prevent a fall from the ledge. Belay anchors are located at this and similar locations in the valley. (Source: Rick Weber, Muir Valley.)

FALL ON ROCK, ATTEMPT TO CLIP BOLT – TOO MUCH SLACK IN ROPE
Red River Gorge, Muir Valley

During the early evening on March 19, a woman (22) was leading the sport route Tanduay Time (5.10d) at the Boneyard Wall and fell while trying to clip the anchors. She fell approximately 20 feet, hitting the prominent ledge about halfway down. She impacted on her lower back and was lowered to the ground by her belayer. She complained of significant back pain. One of her party called Muir Valley Rescue on a nearby emergency-station radio. Rescuers arrived about four minutes later and treated and packaged the patient for litter transport to the Muir Emergency Road, where an ambulance awaited.

Analysis

The general consensus was that there was too much slack in the rope between the belayer and climber. In a re-enactment the next day, a "normal" lead fall from this point on the wall resulted in a modest fall that terminated several feet above the point where the victim impacted the ledge. (Source: Rick Weber, Muir Valley.)

FALL ON ROCK, WEATHER, POOR COMMUNICATION, EXHAUSTION
Red River Gorge

A group of six spent the day of March 21 climbing at the Gallery before heading over to the Playground. Once at the Playground, the climbers set up on two climbs, a 5.10b and a 5.10a. The climber on Jungle Gym (5.10b) was unable to move past the crux and lowered, letting another climber try. The climber was able to make the next clip after the crux (the fourth bolt on the climb, about 25 feet up), but was unable to climb further before the party heard thunder. The climber did not know how to set up a mid-climb bail system, and was lowered.

On the 5.10a, I (GW, 24) instructed the climber who was top-roping the route to finish and clean the climb while I got onto the 10b, set up a bail system, and cleaned our gear. I proceeded to climb to the last bolt and clipped it with a sling and wire-gate carabiner. Then I attempted to construct a bail system I had discussed with an instructor earlier that day, instead of my standard approach. After lowering on the alternative system, it failed to let me pull the rope—the rope got jammed in the bolt hanger. The rope was now in the bolt about 25 feet in the air. The belay side of the rope still had about 40 meters of rope, while the climber's side had about 20 meters.

Assessing the situation, I decided that I could use the belayer side of the rope to lead the climb back to the bolt and fix the jam. I took the tail end of the rope from the belay side, providing me plenty of rope for the climb, and proceeded to climb back up. I made the first bolt and began to work past it, but due to exhaustion I only managed to make it a few feet higher before I began to weaken.

The first bolt is approximately ten feet off the deck, and the second bolt is another eight. I was about two feet from the first bolt; it was near my knees. Fearing a ground-fall if I failed to make the second bolt, I planned to rest and then finish the climb. I asked my belayer to "take," intending to have the slack removed and the belayer close against the wall so that I would take a small fall of about four feet.

The belayer moved into the wall and took slack, as I intended. However, moments before I let go, the belayer asked if I was falling. I responded "Yes!" as I finally slipped and let go. Unfortunately, the belayer proceeded to add a large amount of slack just as I let go. I proceeded to deck and pulled the belayer about three feet off the ground. I landed on my side, but was unhurt, as her dynamic catch softened my landing. My belayer also was unhurt. Following the fall, I completed the climb, cleaned the route, and retreated before the arrival of the storm.

Analysis

The accident resulted from the belayer adding slack, as well as the weight difference between the climber and the lighter belayer. The botched bail system did not contribute to the fall directly, though my exhaustion and the strain of retreat caused my inability to complete the climb. The belayer feared spiking me, and added the slack to soften my catch, a habit brought over from the gym. From this experience, I learned two lessons: Establish a clear standard of communication between belayer and climber, and always wear a helmet. While I had clearly explained what I desired from my belayer, she misunderstood how I wanted her to respond to those commands. And while I had worn my helmet on every other climb of that trip, I had failed to put it on in my rush to clean the system and retreat. Thankfully, it did not make a difference, but the result could have been very different! (Source: Gavin W.)

FALL ON ROCK, CARDIAC ARREST – DEHYDRATION AND LACK OF BLOOD PRESSURE MEDICATION
Red River Gorge, Muir Valley

Late in the afternoon on June 19, a man (44) was climbing a sport route named Earth Surfer (5.11d) in Muir Valley. While on lead about 50 feet up and being belayed by his 15-year-old son, he groaned and went limp as though he had passed out. He then took what would be considered a long, but moderate, fall of about 25 feet. He stopped in air about level with the second bolt, the fall being skillfully arrested by his son.

The victim did not impact the rock face on the way down, nor did he impact the ground. After falling, the victim was hanging limp in his harness and was not moving. His son immediately lowered him to the ground, where other climbers in the area tried unsuccessfully to locate a pulse or detect breathing. Two young men started CPR while another ran to a Muir Emergency Station and radioed for help. Rick Weber, lead WFR, was nearby and arrived at the scene about 10 minutes after the victim fell. He radioed the county dispatcher and requested a helicopter. He then took over administering CPR. Other Muir Valley Rescue volunteers arrived and assisted with CPR for about an hour. After determining that there were no signs of life, efforts at resuscitation were terminated. The medical examiner determined that the victim died of a massive coronary event and that death occurred immediately.

Analysis

The victim's son, who was belaying him, reported that his father had run out of blood pressure medication. The pair had been climbing all day in 90-degree weather on strenuous routes. (Source: Rick Weber.)

FALL ON ROCK, ATTEMPTING TO CLIP BOLT – INADEQUATE PROTECTION, EXCEEDING ABILITIES
Red River Gorge, Muir Valley

On June 16 a man (48) started to climb a sport route called I Banged my ***** Knee. When he got about eight feet off the ground and was attempting to clip the first bolt, he fell and impacted the ground. His fractured his right tibia and fibula. Muir Valley Rescue was called from a nearby emergency-station radio. Volunteers, including three paramedics, responded in about three minutes. The patient was treated, packaged, and transported to an ambulance that was waiting on the Muir Emergency Road.

Analysis

The climber was inexperienced and could have avoided the accident by stick-clipping the first bolt. (Source: Rick Weber.)

FALL ON ROCK, UNFINISHED HARNESS KNOT, DISTRACTION
Red River Gorge, Muir Valley

On October 26 a man (45) with significant rock climbing and paramedic rescue experience fell from a height of about 30 feet, sustaining serious injuries. "I can't tell you how embarrassing it is to have had such an accident," the man reported. "The cause was nothing more than failure to tie in. I remember tying the figure eight and feeding it through my harness, and then I started talking to someone for a few minutes and never followed the knot through. When I started climbing, it appeared as if I was tied in, but I was not. Thankfully, I didn't get nearly as far on the route as I thought I would."

Analysis

It was the last climb on the last day, and our group just lost focus. Climbing is a great sport that can be enjoyed safely. Just make sure everyone is watching out for everyone out there. Check your knots! (Source: Chris Hannes.)

ADDITIONAL NOTES FROM MUIR VALLEY

Ankle injuries were the most common reported in Muir Valley in 2012. There were six that Muir Valley Rescue volunteers responded to. Climbers were treated, transported to their cars, and directed to medical care. Many ankle injuries in this area are the result of a ground fall after a climber fails to clip the first bolt. Stick-clipping the first bolt is strongly recommended for the types of sport climbs here. All of the 300-plus sport routes have their first bolts located near 16 feet, allowing for easy stick-clipping. (Source: Rick Weber.)

MAINE

FALL ON ROCK, SOLO BOULDERING, INEXPERIENCE
Acadia National Park, Monument Cove

Rangers rescued two people seriously injured in separate falling accidents in early June. The first one (not a climbing accident), on June 8, involved a 19-year-old Massachusetts man who was jumping around on the rocks near the summit of Acadia Mountain with friends when he slipped and fell approximately 10 feet off a boulder, then rolled down the steep mountainside for an additional 75 feet. Rangers and the Mount Desert Island SAR team set up a series of low-angle raises and lowers to get him back onto the trail and then down the steep trail to the road. He sustained head trauma, facial injuries, and a broken neck in the fall.

Two days later, on the afternoon of June 10, rangers received a 911 call reporting that a 23-year-old woman had fallen approximately 30 to 35 feet. Upon arrival, they found that the Montana woman had been bouldering the sea stack at Monument Cove, located along the park's rocky shoreline. It was her first time climbing. At a distance of 30 to 35 feet above the ground, she fell from the rock face and landed on the cobblestone beach below.

After a technical rope rescue by park rangers and Mount Desert Island SAR, she was flown from the scene by a Life Flight helicopter. The woman sustained extensive injuries, including a broken neck, a basal skull fracture, a broken collarbone, bilateral ankle fractures, and thoracic bleeding. (Source: Acadia National Park press release, June 14, 2012.)

Analysis

Acadia is a popular climbing area and now sees many visitors in the summer. The young man "jumping around on the rocks" is typical behavior, but is not considered climbing. The young woman clearly got in for more than she bargained. No bouldering pad, no spotters, no experience, but probably lots of exuberance contributed to serious injuries. We have to include it in our data, even though it was her first time climbing. (Source: Jed Williamson.)

FALL ON ROCK, INADEQUATE PROTECTION AT CLIFFTOP
Camden Hills State Park, Mt. Megunticook, Maiden Cliff

Maria Millard (28) was climbing with friends Sigrid Coffin and John Cronin. Moments before she was going to rappel from the top of a climb, her partners recalled her saying, "I'm off belay, I'm safe." She then fell an estimated 65 feet.

Julie Libby of Camden First Aid, which assisted at the scene, said she believes Millard landed on her shoulder on small rocks and hard-packed soil. "It seemed like the brunt of it was on her shoulder and the side of her face," she said. Partner John Cronin said he thought Millard may have lost consciousness for about 30 seconds, but Libby said the woman was conscious during the half-hour it took to lower her down the mountain, and she was speaking coherently, suggesting she did not sustain a serious head injury. She was wearing a helmet. (Source: Edited from an article in *Bangor Daily News*, October 12, 2012, by Tom Groening.)

Analysis

Millard is fortunate in terms of the level of injuries she sustained after a long fall. It would seem that her category of cause has to do with switching from being on belay to preparing for a rappel at the top of a climb. This can be a vulnerable time, but one can secure to an anchor with a sling while setting up for a rappel. (Source: Jed Williamson.)

MASSACHUSETTS

FALL ON ROCK, INADEQUATE BELAY – CAM DEVICE OPEN, NO BACKUP KNOTS
Hammond Pond, Vittles Wall

On April 14 I was climbing Hominey (5.8) on the Vittles Wall, a 25-foot crag near Hammond Pond. I've been climbing for five years, and although I have easily completed routes rated more difficult than this, I have struggled and fallen repeatedly on the crux bulge at the top of Hominey. Although I was without a partner, I had a few free hours that morning and was in the area, so I decided to take another shot at Hominey on self-belay.

I was using a Petzl Basic on a fixed line. The Petzl Basic documentation warns that the cam that locks on the rope can be jammed by foreign material and fail to close. Petzl recommends tying backup knots on a redundant line. Having repeatedly fallen on my Basic over the previous year without mishap, I neglected to tie backup knots. On other occasions I had felt that spending time and energy tying these knots weakened me just as I needed strength for hard moves.

This time I easily reached the crux but, as usual, struggled to get over it. Twice, I decided to downclimb to a rest just below the bulge. Both times I had to open the cam on the Basic to allow the rope to pass through the device. On the third attempt, I popped off my holds and heard the rope whip through the device without any resistance. I had enough time during the fall to realize that, although it was unlikely that I would die, this would be a serious accident.

I landed on my left foot. The impact felt incredibly violent, and I could tell immediately that I had broken my left tibial plateau badly. I stood on my right leg to disconnect myself from the rope, and lay down to call 911. I had taken a wilderness first-aid course two years ago, and realized that blood circulation was important for the survival of my leg, so I straightened it into a position of function. The Vittles Wall is a bit off the beaten path, so I was on the phone for 45 minutes while the Newton firefighters looked for me. Eventually the 911 dispatcher suggested I yell to help them locate me. Another climber heard me yell and led the firefighters in my direction.

The Newton firefighters did an incredible job carrying me out on a board. I spent the next 52 days in Beth Israel Hospital in Boston. I've had 13 surgeries, two metal plates, too many screws to count, and a post-op infection for nearly a year. I might need knee replacement surgery.

Analysis

I'm not sure why the cam did not close. It's possible that the tip of my belt managed to get into it and hold it open. It's also possible that after the second downclimb I left it locked in the open position, which is possible with the Basic. (Source: Streph Treadway, 44.)

(Editor's note: She mentioned not tying backup knots, but did not indicate whether they would have prevented grounding out. They may well have. Also of note is a recurring theme: the value of having taken a wilderness first-aid course.)

MONTANA

FALL ON ROCK, INADEQUATE BELAY, INADEQUATE PROTECTION
Gallatin Canyon, Gallatin Tower

On September 18, Jacob van Almelo (25) was climbing the route Tigger (5.10a/b) when he fell at the crux move. His 30-foot fall resulted in several injuries. His belayer did not catch the fall, but protection pulling out may also have had something to do with the length of the fall.

The Gallatin County Sheriff's Office, Big Sky Fire Department, and Gallatin County Search and Rescue responded to the scene. Members of the Big Sky Fire Department hiked in and stabilized the climber until members of the Gallatin County Search and Rescue arrived.

Van Almelo reportedly sustained a minor laceration on his head and possible fractures on his lower legs. He was immobilized and transported by ambulance to Bozeman Deaconess Hospital by the Big Sky Fire Department. (Source: Edited from a posting on the website of KSLF.com, Bozeman News, on September 19, 2012.)

(Editor's note: Although the details are sparse, it is interesting to see a posting from a climbing area that rarely makes it into this publication.)

NEVADA

FALL ON ROCK, INEXPERIENCE, WEATHER
Red Rock, Pine Creek Canyon, Cat in the Hat

On April 5, a young woman (early 20s, I think) fell about 20 feet (though no one knows for sure because there were no witnesses) while being lowered by her husband off the first pitch of Cat in the Hat (6 pitches, 5.6). She sustained a head injury. She was conscious and lucid throughout her evacuation.

Two climbers not associated with the couple arrived at the scene right after the accident and administered first aid, and one of them went to the parking area to get a cell phone and call for help. Shortly after that, my friends and I rappelled off the route and into the scene, and first learned of the accident. We hiked out partway to help SAR and the EMTs get to the accident victim, who was still being tended to by her husband and another climber. At this point it was dark.

The SAR crew, the EMTs, and four of us bystanding climbers then carried the victim to a location where a helicopter could get to her. The EMTs got the call around 6:30 p.m., and she was airlifted around 9 or 9:30 p.m. (Source: Edited from a post on Mountainproject.com by "kBobby.")

Analysis

The winds were extremely high that afternoon, with gusts to 60 mph in the area. (I estimate the gusts on Cat in the Hat were around 40 mph.) This is probably a contributing factor in their decision to lower instead of rappel during some of their descent. The winds abated around 9 p.m., which allowed the helicopter to come in.

My three friends and I had crossed paths with this couple about two hours earlier, at the top of the third pitch (where all the slings are around the block), while we were still going up and they were going down. Ominously, as she was rappelling from the top of the third pitch, the victim said to my friend, "I'm glad you are here so that if we get stuck you can rescue us." My friend told me this as we were rappelling down the first pitch, moments before we got to the bottom and found out that the girl was injured. My friend also told me this climb was the couple's first multi-pitch climb and their second trad climb.

Earlier, before we had caught up to them at the third-pitch belay, another party told us that one of the two had dropped a belay device and that they were both having an unhappy time.

One of the climbers who arrived on the scene first said that he thought she was being lowered, then stopped on a ledge while slack was still being paid out, then fell.

From another posting on Mountain Project by "Rockwood:" I am one of kBobby's friends and was climbing with him the day of the accident; I'm the one the injured climber talked to at the belay near the top when she asked about being rescued. I'm also the one almost hit by her falling ATC while sitting at the second belay. To clarify some of his details, she did get her ATC back. It landed near me at the tree on the top of the second pitch. We found it and my partner brought it up to her as we climbed up. At the slings (top of the third pitch) she was rapping, not being lowered, so don't worry about the rings. It wasn't until the last pitch that the lowering happened, and at that point they were on bolt anchors. It was very windy and she was very cold and extremely sketched out and panicky. I was doing my best to calm her down with chitchat as my partner climbed, and that's when I discovered how inexperienced they were.

The ability to remain calm is critical in preventing accidents. The foreshadowing of this event was unbelievable, but I was glad we were there to help direct the rescue workers and hope she's doing better. I'm considering a WFR class as well after this.

FALL ON ROCK, INADEQUATE PROTECTION
Red Rock, Calico Basin, Big Bad Wolf

On April 7 around 3 p.m., my partner and I had just finished Physical Graffiti and were at the base of the route and packing up to leave. I was watching two guys struggle on Big Bad Wolf (5.9). The climber was just about to clip what I believe was the fourth bolt and didn't make it. He swung down and hit the wall with one foot twisted. He immediately yelled that he had broken his ankle. I assisted the belayer in lowering the climber to where I could reach him, then positioned him to protect his bad ankle. I grabbed him and was able to hold him up with his arm around my neck. I asked if anyone had a cell phone, and an off-duty sheriff with search and rescue, who was also packing up to leave, came up. We laid the climber down and he took over. He assessed the climber for other injuries, splinted his ankle, and asked if he could walk out, to which he said no. The sheriff located a good landing area nearby and called in a helicopter.

Analysis

There are two things I took away from this rescue, which may be obvious now but were not at the time. The first was to assess the total condition of the injured person. He wasn't hurt anywhere else, but it would have been easy for me to overlook it. Take the extra two minutes to step back and fully assess the individual.

The second is something the sheriff said several times when we were handling or moving the injured person: "Do not hurry." It's pretty easy to get excited and rush, and end up making things worse. Take your time, moving carefully through obstacles to make sure no one sustains further injury. (Source: From a post on Mountainproject.com by "rging.")

STRANDED, OFF-ROUTE, DARKNESS, INEXPERIENCE
Red Rock, Black Velvet Canyon

On July 3 around 8 a.m., two climbers visiting from Ohio made the approach to the base of Epinephrine, a 5.9, 15-pitch route located in Black Velvet Canyon. In addition to their climbing equipment, they had five liters of water. As the day progressed, they lost the route on several occasions. They consumed their last bit of water at 4 p.m. As the sun set, they began coming to the realization that they might be in trouble. By 11 p.m., they knew they needed help. They eventually found a ledge where they were able to get cell phone reception and made the call.

At 12:30 a.m. on July 4, our unit received the call, and five officers were immediately dispatched to the area. They assessed the situation and determined that a technical rescue was needed. Volunteers received the call at 2:30 a.m. and met at the Cottonwood parking lot. Officers began setting up systems while the volunteers were en route. As volunteers arrived, they boarded the helicopter and were flown to Black Velvet Peak.

One officer was immediately lowered to the climbers, who were on a ledge approximately 400 feet below the peak. One volunteer was also lowered to help in recovering the two stranded climbers. Over the course of the next five hours, both climbers were raised back to the peak. At one point, sleet came down on the team, followed by heavy rain.

Both climbers were safely delivered to their vehicle, having learned that five liters of water just wasn't enough and that route planning is crucial, especially in an unfamiliar environment.

They did, however, do a couple of things right. They told people where they were going, and when they found they were in trouble, they stayed put and called for help. Even if they weren't able to get cell reception, their friends knew they were overdue, knew where they were, and would have been able to call for help on their behalf. (Source: Edited from a posting on the Las Vegas Metropolitan Police Department Search and Rescue Unit blog: lvmpdsar.blogspot.com.)

From a post on the same blog by John Wilder: "We're always happy to have a positive outcome! A fair number of people lose the route when they leave the top of the tower. If they had headed up the Original Velvet Route, then thought they were supposed to go straight up rather than up and right, that would get them to roughly 400 feet below the peak and in deep crap."

NEW HAMPSHIRE

AVALANCHE, POOR POSITION, WEATHER
Mt. Washington, Huntington Ravine

On January 5 a party of two was climbing Central Gully when the leader was hit with a naturally triggered sluff avalanche. During the resulting fall, one of the climbers fractured his ankle. Much of the information below was gathered from a narrative provided by a guide who was in the area, as well as from conversations with the injured party.

Just prior to the incident, the guided group climbed up to top of the ice bulge in Central Gully. The guide decided not to continue up due to excessive spindrift, blowing snow, and generally harsh conditions above treeline. He had a three–ice screw anchor built for his group in the ice. When the party of two arrived, he allowed them to clip the anchor while they climbed the ice. However, after the group cleared the ice, they were climbing unprotected with a short rope between them.

At this point the guide was at the top belay, out of the fall line, while his clients were down at an ice screw anchor below the ice, also out of the fall line. About 15 meters above the ice, the party of two was hit with a loose snow (sluff) avalanche that carried them both downslope. According to the leader, the force felt as though he had received a stiff push or kick in the chest. The guide heard, "Avalanche!" but did not see the falling climbers pass by. He descended to his clients to get them situated. He assumed that the slide had happened below him, and that the party of two was still up in the gully. About 10 minutes later he heard a call for help. The party had fallen about 100 meters, coming to rest about 30 meters below a fracture line from two days earlier. The second climber had sustained an ankle injury. The lead climber was uninjured but broke his climbing helmet in the fall. It wasn't until the guide descended to the injured party that he learned it was the climbers above him who had been avalanched past.

With help from his clients and the partner of the injured climber, the guide was able to lower the patient toward the bottom of the fan. At this point two clients went to the rescue cache to bring up a litter. The guide had been able to wrap the patient in a bivy bag and help keep him warm with a water bottle of hot tea placed between his legs. The patient was placed in the litter, and they worked their way down to the Harvard Cabin. From the time of the accident (2 p.m.) to the time they arrived at the cabin was about four hours. Their efforts were very much appreciated, since the trail from the bottom of the fan to the cabin was very difficult for a litter carry in the lean snow conditions. U.S. Forest Service snow rangers met the group at the Harvard Cabin, reassessed and resplinted the injured leg, and put the patient in a new litter. They sledded him down the Sherburne Ski Trail, with help from Mountain Rescue Service and students from SOLO who were at Pinkham Notch for a Wilderness First Responder course.

We received word afterward that the patient did indeed break his ankle, which required surgical repair.

Analysis

This day (January 5) was the first 5-scale avalanche advisory for Huntington Ravine that season. The advisory indicated Huntington Ravine started the day at low danger, but moved into the moderate rating as a forecasted one to three inches loaded in on west and northwest winds. The summit recorded 2.4 inches of new snow on January 5, with winds averaging 56 mph.

In our experience looking at avalanche accidents and close calls on Mt. Washington over the years, constant themes, mistakes, and oversights arise. Many of them are related to human psychological factors, the mental drivers that whisper over our shoulder, "Everything is fine, go ahead and have fun, you've done this before," while others miss the bull's-eye data that Mother Nature is offering, not having as much avalanche knowledge as we all should. These are traps any of us can fall into, which highlights how important it is to approach avalanche terrain with skepticism and keep asking the critical questions. (Source: Mountwashingtonavalanchecenter.org.)

(*Editor's note: Two days earlier, two skiers triggered a R2D1.5 avalanche in Central Gully at 2:30 p.m. The previous night, 2.9 inches of new snow had fallen on the summit, accompanied by strong winds. During the morning and through the day, this snow was transported into the deposition area below the Central Gully ice bulge. Both Tuckerman and Huntington ravines were under a general advisory identifying snow-stability concerns in isolated snowfields.)*

SLIP ON ICE, NO CRAMPONS, PROBABLY FATIGUE
Mt. Adams

On January 10, Gregory Frux (53) and Matt Burd (52), who had climbed Mt. Tripyramid North Peak the previous day, were joined by Nick Jaques (52) for a mountaineering adventure. They ascended the Lowes Path for 3,000 vertical feet to the Grey Knob RMC Hut, encountering icy trails and using crampons the entire way. The following morning they attempted Mt. Adams, second-highest point in New England at 5,774 feet, via the Spur Trail. Conditions above treeline were fair, with snowdrifts and blowing snow. Visibility declined to near whiteout conditions, and the party was insecure about routefinding. At 5,200 feet they turned back and safely returned to Grey Knob Hut for another night. The following morning, in good weather, they descended via the Hincks Trail, a more gentle descent. Travel was fast, and they reconnected with Lowes Path via the King Ravine Trail. At this junction they decided to remove their crampons, because the terrain had minimal snow cover and travel was on frozen mud, rocks, and some ice.

A short distance beyond this point, at 2,300 feet, Matt slipped and was hurt trying to stop his fall. The party assessed the lower left leg, below the knee joint. They agreed Matt should not remove his mountaineering boot, and Nick splinted the limb with two birch branches and duct tape built around the boot. Matt first determined that he could stand and second that he could walk with the support of two ski poles. Based on map and altimeter readings, they estimated they were a little over a mile from the road and about 900 feet above it. Given that it was 12:30 p.m., they agreed that self-rescue was possible. Matt hobbled and slid down the trail for the next four hours, while Greg and Nick shuttled his pack forward. Several stops were made for water, tea, and food. They reached the car at 4:30 p.m. At the hospital Matt was diagnosed with a fractured fibula, which was minimally displaced.

Analysis

Wearing or not wearing 12-point crampons at the place we removed them was a judgment call, since there was some hazard to each option. Matt's attending physician suggested use of micro-spikes as a good alternative. One contributory factor may have been relaxation of attention near the end of the hike.

The team was well satisfied with the choices made after the rescue was initiated and felt they worked very well together. The amount of time involved in self-rescue was surprisingly long, and would have become a much more serious problem had the accident happened higher on the mountain. (Source: Edited from a report sent in by Gregory Frux.)

(Editor's note: The White Mountains in winter are considered to be a serious

mountaineering environment. Winter incidents are usually above timberline, but the trails can require climbing equipment and technique.)

FALL ON ROCK, OFF-ROUTE, UNABLE TO CLIP TO PROTECTION
Rumney, 5.8 Crag

On May 18 a Dartmouth Outing Club excursion to Rumney included nine climbers. When they arrived, they split into teams and went to their selected climbs, having agreed to meet back at the van in early evening.

Lynn (20s) had been climbing with her partner at 5.8 Crag at the same time that Anna's beginner trip (a separate group) happened to be climbing there. Lynn was leading a sport route when she got a little off-route, failed to secure a clipping hold, and fell. She glanced off a small ledge, taking the impact mostly on her lower back. It was painful, and she lowered off the route. Anna, who was nearby, saw this happen and helped to make sure Lynn was OK. Anna's beginner trip was heading home anyway, so Lynn had plenty of company as she walked back to our parked van. Her walking was apparently slow and pained.

Once I reached the van and learned what had happened from both Lynn and Anna, I asked Lynn if I could check her over again. I asked her about the pain, palpated her spine, etc. I thought it would be OK to drive her back to Hanover in the van as planned, but asked if she would rather take an ambulance, which she refused. We got her in the most comfortable position we could (lying on her back) and made our way back to Hanover, where I brought her and her climbing partner to the ER at Hitchcock upon her request. She was fully aware, laughing, etc., but I believe that she wanted to get some X-rays taken to make sure there was no serious damage. Eventually the doctors confirmed that there were no broken bones or other serious issues. They told Lynn to rest the area and take an anti-inflammatory. I brought Lynn and her partner back to campus, where Lynn said she felt fine to be on her own. I called her the next day to check in, and she seemed to be recovering fine.

Analysis

Lynn and her partner were both relatively new to sport leading. Both were wearing helmets. She and her partner had all the knowledge and resources they needed in order to deal with the situation on their own, but because Rumney is a busy place, there were plenty of people around to help, including multiple groups of DOC and other Dartmouth undergrads.

Anna Morenz has a Wilderness EMT certification, I have a Wilderness First Responder certification, and multiple others on the Rumney van and in Anna's beginner trip had other medical certifications.

Overall I would say this event was within the normal range of accidents to be expected while sport climbing, and that the response was appropriate. I think that Lynn and her partner were climbing responsibly, that Anna and I responded responsibly, that the DOC's policies were effective, and that the situation was resolved in the best possible way. (Source: John Thompson, DOC trip leader.)

(Editor's note: First, this climbing area is very popular. Many more incidents occur

here each year, but we don't hear about them—unless they are fatalities or injuries requiring outside assistance—because the climbers, as in this case, self-rescue. Second, I specifically asked the DOC for this report because it is an excellent example of self-reporting and competence on the part of the climbers and leaders.)

NEW YORK

FALL ON ICE, CLIMBING UNROPED, INEXPERIENCED
Adirondack Mountains, Nippletop

On December 15 the weather in the northern Adirondack Mountains was bluebird clear but cold. I had spent the day with a fellow New York State Department of Environmental Conservation (DEC) forest ranger patrolling on foot to the 2,000-foot summit of Hamlin Mountain in Essex County. At 10 a.m. the same day, four men (no names, ages, or level of experience provided) from Syracuse, New York, began ascending Nippletop Mountain in the Dix Mountain Wilderness via a technical climb up a natural slide on the mountain's west side. Three of the men were experienced mountaineers, and the fourth was not. They had decided prior to beginning the climb that they wouldn't use a rope or other protection until one of them felt uncomfortable.

They were wearing climbing helmets and using ice axes and crampons to make their way up the ice-covered slide. Around 4 p.m., when the four were three-quarters of the way up the slide, one of them reached a point where he felt he needed to be roped in. He communicated this to his climbing partners, who were above him.

While one of the men above attempted to get into position to lower a rope to him, the three above saw their partner who had called for the rope begin to first slide and then cartwheel down the stair-step, ice-covered slide. According to one report, the novice climber seemed to "just let go." He made no attempt to self-arrest with his ice axe. The climber fell 200 feet down the slide before coming to a stop against a log frozen in the ice. The other climbers could hear their friend moaning and observed him moving his arms. He began to slide again, and went another 20 feet until he was stopped by small trees growing on the slide.

His friends made a quick plan. One would rappel down and stay with the victim, providing whatever assistance he could. The other two would quickly climb to the summit and call 911 on their cell phone. (One of the men had made a call home from the mountain's summit during the summer.) They provided the climber who was staying with an insulated jacket and whatever other clothes they could quickly hand off for the victim. The two climbers reached the top of the slide and then bushwhacked to the summit, but were unable to get cell service in either location. They hurried down the trail but could not make a call until they reached town.

My state cell phone rang, and the caller ID showed it was the DEC Dispatch in Ray Brook. The dispatcher advised me of accident and asked me to contact two climbers at the Noonmark Diner in Keene Valley. I arrived at the diner at 8:30

p.m. and met with the two very upset climbers inside. They once again described what happened. They stated that they were sure they saw the victim's arm move at one point, and they definitely heard him moaning.

At 10:30 p.m. two other rangers, a physician's assistant, and I left the command post and began hiking toward the injured climber. We carried all the equipment needed to stabilize and protect the climber until first light, when a helicopter could fly in. We hiked the trail to Elk Pass and then followed the tracks the climbers had made early in the day when they bushwhacked to the slide. As we came out near the slide we spotted the headlight of the climber who had stayed with the injured man. Although it looked like only short distance above us through the woods, it took us an hour to reach the two men. We arrived at the location at 3:30 a.m. on December 16. The physician's assistant began assessing, stabilizing, and warming the injured climber with assistance from forest rangers. He had multiple skull fractures, intercranial pressure, fractured C1, broken ribs, and a six-inch-long laceration on his left cheek. He was also hypothermic.

At 4:20 a.m. six forest rangers geared up and left the command post to head to our location. At the same time another ranger was in the State Police helicopter hangar at the Lake Clear Airport, 20 miles away, preparing the helicopter for a hoist operation. The weather window was small but appeared to provide enough time to fly in, lower a litter, move away, and then return to hoist the patient and the physician's assistant out. However, the helicopter was not even able to get close enough for those of us on the ground to ever hear it. At that point I knew we were about to begin one of the most difficult and grueling carry-outs that DEC forest rangers have done in recent memory.

At 8:30 a.m. the six forest rangers arrived with the litter for the carry-out, and shortly after that two experienced local climbers that had been asked to assist in the rescue operation joined us. A discussion ensued regarding the best route for the carry. It was decided to use a rope belay system to lower the injured climber five pitches, each about 200 feet in length, to the bottom of the slide. We would then carry him up through a spruce-fir forest to Elk Pass, where we could pick up the Nippletop Mountain Trail. We could then use a backpack carry system for the remaining one and a half miles down the trail to the vehicles.

We began carrying at 8:30 a.m. but did not reach the ambulance waiting at the command post until 8 p.m. Eleven and a half hours of carrying, sliding, dragging, lifting, pulling, cutting, throwing, and pushing by forest rangers, volunteer climbers, and local emergency response volunteers.

Once we reached the bottom of the slide, we had to carry the litter through the spruce-fir forest. Again we worked in teams with a group of forest rangers using axes and handsaws to clear a trail while the other group would carry the litter. When we arrived at the trail, we rigged up the backpack carry system. Once we reached the Ausable Club Road, we loaded the litter on one of the vehicles and drove out to meet an ambulance from the Keene Valley Rescue Squad. The injured climber was transported to the local hospital and then on to Fletcher Allen Hospital in Burlington, Vermont, where he was operated on immediately. Intercranial pressure was the biggest concern. He is making a slow recovery, but his doctor feels he will recover and return to his family members and friends. (Source: New York State Forest Ranger Rob Praczkajlo.)

FALL ON ROCK, PROTECTION PULLED
Mohonk Preserve, Shawangunks, Birdland

On May 26 I was attempting to climb Birdland, which ascends the right side of a beautiful open book corner. As you traverse out right, you can clip a couple of older, large, angle pitons that are commonly found in the Gunks. These are much more substantial pitons than you will find at Seneca, and many have been replaced over the years.

After moving past the corner and bulge with the pitons, I worked up to the crux moves at a shallow, right-facing corner. There was an old pin scar directly above and some small cracks above and slightly left. Looking for a placement (at this point about five feet plus above my last piece), I found the crescent-shaped crack/pin scar and placed a purple (#0) Master Cam vertically. From what I could see, the two front lobes were cammed perfectly. What I could not see were the two rear lobes. I wrongly assumed they were cammed the same as the front lobes. After several attempts to figure out the crux moves to the left, I stepped back down toward my piece and prepared to hang. I yelled "Take!" and sat back, and bam—the piece blew out, and down I went for a nice ride.

As I was in free fall for a split second, my hand inadvertently reached out and grabbed the rope. It was completely reactionary, and I almost immediately let go. I did, however, receive a minor burn across my hand. The piece of protection below me was one of the old pitons, which held. Thankfully it was a clean fall and Mitch (my belayer) gave a nice catch. At that point, it was a mental battle to get back up there, but I eventually did. I hung there while someone threw me some tape so I could protect my hand. I got back on (backed up the piton this time), made two much better placements consisting of a brass offset and a BD C3 (not in the pin scar), hung on that, fell on that, and then finally worked through the crux exclaiming, "Seriously? You've got to be kidding me... That's all it was?!"

The second pitch was wonderful, and I made sure to do the 5.9 overhang variation.

Analysis

This was not the first time I'd had a piece of gear blow out on me, but it hadn't happened since I was a very young and more naive trad leader. Looking back, this was an incident that should never have happened, but it provided me with some exceedingly useful lessons, and for that I'm grateful. Lessons learned:

1. Make sure of those cam placements, especially with the smaller sizes. They can rip out more easily than the larger sizes, especially when your placement is half-crap. I should never have blindly trusted the placement, assuming that the inside of the crack was the same as the outer portion. The back two lobes were probably wide open.

2. Back up those old pitons if you use them, if at all possible. If that piton

had blown, it would probably have been "game over" for me, or serious injuries at the least.

3. Give yourself all the time you need after a fall to collect yourself and figure out if you want to continue. There's nothing that says you have to continue, and I'm glad to know that I thought it through and decided to finish the route.

4. Whatever you decide to do, commit 100 percent to it. Reaching the end of the pitch after that battle was one of the highlights of my summer, and pulling the overhang at the end of pitch two was worth all the struggles on pitch one. It only happened because, once I made up my mind to continue, I was completely focused on that task. (Source: Andy Weinmann, 34.)

FALLS ON ROCK (7), RAPPEL ERRORS (4), POOR POSITION (3), EXCEEDING ABILITIES (3), INADEQUATE BELAY, INADEQUATE PROTECTION, NO HELMET, CLIMBING UNROPED
Mohonk Preserve, Shawangunks

Fifteen reports from the Gunks were submitted for 2012, not including the previous incident.

There was only one fatality, on April 29, when the anchor system at the top of Easy Keyhole (5.2) failed as Stephanie Prezant (22) was about to be lowered. When she weighted the system—six or so slings around a tree—it came away. (No details as to why or how.) She fell 20 feet and struck her head. She was not wearing a helmet.

The other rappel errors were attributed to 1) one end of the rappel rope slipping through the device, 2) a simul-rappel in which the weights of the rappellers were uneven, and 3) "an error in the rappel set-up" that resulted in a ground fall and fractures.

The average age of the climbers was 31, and the average degree of difficulty of the climbs was 5.6. One man (50) suffered cardiac arrest while he was climbing, resulting in his death following CPR and a litter carry-out. This unfortunate incident is not counted as a climbing accident. (Source: From reports submitted by Mohonk Preserve and Jeremiah Horrigan in a local newspaper.)

NORTH CAROLINA

FALL ON ROCK, INADEQUATE PROTECTION
Rumbling Bald

During the early afternoon of January 2, Bill McAfee (40) fell off Good Samaritans (5.9+), located on the Cereal Buttress. He had placed a solid-looking No. 3 Camalot about 10 to 12 feet into the climb. He climbed another 10 feet or so, and was working on placing another piece of pro. McAfee and his partner had discussed using the bolts on an adjacent route (Frankenberry), but they were out of reach. He was approximately 25 to 30 feet up the corner, doing a layback move, when he fell.

McAfee experienced severe head trauma despite wearing a helmet. Rescue personnel, working with climbers, carried him down from the Cereal Buttress to the parking lot. A helicopter left around 3:10 p.m. He died later in the day.

Analysis

Bill McAfee climbed too far above his last piece of protection for it to even matter in the event of a fall. He was too run-out. (Source: Aram Attarian.)

FALL ON ROCK, FAILURE TO FOLLOW ROUTE
Rumbling Bald

On February 25, I (Mike Best, no age given) arrived at Rumbling Bald around 7:50 a.m. to meet John, my partner for the day. We started with Comatose (5.8), followed by an unnamed sport climb (5.9).

After completing both climbs we elected to do Bunky's Rest Day (5.8). Neither of us had done the route before, but based on the topo and rating, it seemed to be a route that I could easily climb. The topo shows twin cracks leading straight up to a slab, then moves out to a bolt (5.8). From this point the route moves up and right to a second bolt, then over a small roof and on to the anchors. The total climb to the anchors is 150 feet.

I racked up, John put me on belay, and I headed up the twin cracks. The climbing to start isn't terribly difficult (5.6), with tricky but ample gear placements. After 50 feet I plugged a finger-size cam and moved out to the first bolt. I clipped the bolt at a ledge and took my first assessment of the upper part of the route, which wasn't visible from the ground.

At this point I realized the route gets more serious. From here I could barely see the second bolt. Moving between the first and the second bolt definitely takes you through a no-fall area, because the farther right you climb, the more likely you become to fall directly into the gully, which has several ledges and trees that could definitely cause injury.

The second bolt featured another nice rest area with a small ledge and good handhold. This was a good area for another risk assessment. From here, bailing was very easy; I could be lowered to a rappel station in the gully, or could elect to rappel off the single bolt (which clearly had been done before as there was a quick-link attached to it). I took a look up the next part of the climb, which involved moving up the slab, pulling the small roof, and then climbing an undetermined distance to the anchor. I could see the roof had several cracks underneath to provide good gear, and the distance to the roof was pretty short.

On my way to the roof, John let me know that we'd reached the center mark on the rope. I was able to move through the roof with a solid undercling, allowing me to get my feet high and reach up for a crimpy hold. Looking up after the roof, I noticed what appeared to be a thin crack no more than 10 feet above, but still no anchor in sight. From here I made the decision to climb the crack, place some gear, and then make another decision. The climbing was definitely a bit tougher, composed of slab moves with poor handholds. Once at the small crack, I realized just how thin it was and placed a Black Diamond C3 (size 0, green). From this point there was no anchor in sight, which meant I was now probably 120 feet up (or 30 feet from the anchor, per the topo). I took a quick look around to find my next point of protection and couldn't find anything. From what I could tell, the route flattened out about 15 feet from where I was, and I assumed a few more feet took you to an anchor. Given that I'd placed a solid piece of gear, I continued up, looking for the anchor.

Immediately after the green cam the climbing got tough—frankly much too tough for a 5.8 climb. I found myself using dime-thick crimps and smears for several moves. About 10 feet out from the green cam, I was still balanced precariously with no anchor in sight, and at this point had no ability to downclimb back to the green cam. I looked left and noticed that if I could move slightly up and left, there was a ledge and some reasonable handholds—in all likelihood the correct route. I moved higher and found myself in a funky position with my left hand and left foot matched on a foothold, right hand on a sidepull, and right foot effectively off the wall. I tried to move more weight onto my left foot, but got nowhere. I was 15 feet above my last piece, and I'd climbed myself right into a place where I couldn't go up and I couldn't downclimb.

I attempted to shift my weight, my left foot smear couldn't take it, and off I went. Sliding feet-first down the slab. I quickly reached the 0 cam and continued over the roof. After I cleared the roof, the rope began to tighten, and eventually I came to a stop right atop the last bolt I'd clipped.

I was effectively lying face-down on the slab, with no weight on my feet and thankful that the fall had stopped. I did a quick personal assessment and tried to get on my feet. That is when I realized I hadn't escaped this fall unscathed. The pain was immediate. On a 1-to-10 scale, this was a 10, easily the most intense pain I'd ever felt, and I realized that standing was not an option. I yelled down to John that I was OK and just needed a minute to collect myself. I attempted to put a little more weight on my right foot, then tried my left foot. Neither was going to work. My back was also in pain, but I had full feeling in my legs, could move everything around, and realized the back injury was just a large bruise from where the harness had come tight. I told John that I couldn't put any weight on either of my feet, and that my back had some pain, but otherwise I was good.

Given my situation, location, and gear, John and I decided that he would lower me to the rappel station. He began lowering, and when I arrived at that last bolt that I'd clipped I told John to hold up. I unclipped my alpine draw, figuring the more slings I had the better. The rest of the lower was relatively easy, although definitely not pain-free, as I was using my hands and my knees to keep myself off the wall. I arrived at the rappel station with 10 feet of rope to spare (whew!), sat myself upright on the slope next to the tree, rigged a tether (using my cordelette and a locking carabiner) to attach myself securely to the tree, and told John I was safe and to take me off belay.

I quickly rigged a rappel with a backup, tossed the rope down, and away I went on a butt-sliding rappel down a gully thick with vegetation. After another 50 feet or so, I arrived 10 feet left of where I'd started the climb and safely on the ground. Estimated time since the fall was about 30 minutes.

Getting down was the easy part—getting to the car was a whole different ball game. Three of John's friends, who had been climbing nearby, offered assistance. (If you think climbers aren't a supportive group, you've clearly not met the right climbers.) One of them, an EMT, immediately began taking off my climbing shoes and gave me some ibuprofen to help deal with the pain.

The scramble down to the main trail wasn't without its pain and awkwardness. As I slid on my rear end, I think I managed to roll over every stump and pointy rock on the trail. After about an hour we arrived at base of the main trail, and three hours after leaving the rock we reached the parking lot of Rumbling Bald.

At the hospital in Charlotte, I was diagnosed with a left calcaneus fractured in three places and a fractured right talus bone. The orthopedist thought that in four to five weeks my right foot should heal enough to allow weight to be placed on it, and that my left foot would take around 10 weeks to bear weight.

Analysis

I got lost on a route that I'd never climbed, and that the guidebook didn't describe in detail. This is a risk I accepted then and accept now. Getting off-route happens, and falls happen. In this case, if I had gone left from the last piece of gear, I would have found easier climbing, likely would've made it to the anchors just fine, and would've climbed a few more routes that day. Having the ability to self-rescue was good. (Source: Mike Best.)

FALL ON ROCK – LOST BALANCE, PROTECTION PULLED OUT
Crowders Mountain State Park, Two-Pitch Wall

I was guiding a group at Gumbies on April 14 when a woman came up from the gully that leads down to Two Pitch Wall to tell me that Chris Bernick (37) had taken a long fall on Secret Service (5.10+)/Double Naught Spy (5.9 R), rendering him unconscious.

From the top of the gully we could see him unconscious on a ledge, extremely far below the piece that had caught him. Chris' buddy was coming up the gully, on his way to the top to try to rappel down to Chris. We followed the friend and assisted with anchoring a rope at the top of the climb, barely reaching Chris.

At this point rescuers arrived, and Alberto Beani, a former Italian mountain rescue team member, was on his way up to Chris, who had fallen to a point approximately 10 feet above the ground. My co-instructor and I fixed the rope at the top so Alberto could clip into it and assess Chris.

Alberto attached himself to the rope and then secured himself to Chris' harness. Chris' belayer, Leslie, and others who had been instructed to hold onto her harness to support her, then lowered the pair to the ground.

According to other climbers at the scene, Chris had reached the crux almost at the top of the climb when he fell. A witness stated that Chris lost his balance while clipping into a cam he had just placed. The fall caused some of his gear below to pull. He fell backward approximately 40 feet and slammed into the rock face head-on, damaging his helmet. He bounced again and landed on the small ledge where he was found unconscious and bleeding profusely. His fall was arrested by a nut (size unknown). Leslie stated that she did not believe she could lower him to the ground by herself without causing further injury, so she chose to wait for help. Chris' fall had pulled her four feet off the ground. Chris sustained severe head trauma and an injury to the right shoulder. He was transported by helicopter to Charlotte Medical Center. (Source: Joe V. and Crowders Mountain State Park.)

Analysis

Great effort and support by climbers assisting climbers. Solid gear placements and an anchored belayer could have made the difference here. (Source: Aram Attarian.)

FALL ON ROCK, PLACED NO OR INADEQUATE PROTECTION
Whiteside Mountain

On May 26, my partner Amanda (24) and I (Ryan, 20) started the day with the intent of climbing Catholic School Girls Direct (5.11), but after completing the first pitch we decided to switch to the Original Route (5.10d), which I'd done before. After I led the first and second pitch, my partner started up the third.

Around 11 a.m., after completing a short traverse and starting to climb off a ledge using a flake that cuts up and left, Amanda's foot slipped. There wasn't any protection placed, so she fell eight feet and landed on a three- to four-foot-wide, down-sloping ledge. Upon impact with the ledge, she heard both her ankles "snap." At this point she was about 80 feet above me, out of sight, and roughly 300 feet off the ground.

After realizing what had happened, I instructed her to pull herself to a position on the ledge where I could take her off belay. Once she did this, I soloed the pitch to get to her. I removed her pack and excess gear and placed it on the ledge. I found some sticks and tape and splinted both her ankles. I then managed to build an anchor to the right and rig our single rope for a rappel. I then clipped our belay loops together with a sling and had her hold onto my neck while I supported her feet with one hand and managed the rappel with the other. I held her across my chest while I rappelled, using a Reverso autoblock backup.

Once reaching the tree ledge on top of the second pitch, I pulled the rope and carried her to the opposite side of the ledge. I located the rappel tree and knew that I would be able to reach the ground from this point. I tied our only rope to the tree with a figure-8 follow-through to make roughly a 200-foot single-rope rappel, and repeated the same rappel procedure as before. Once on the ground, I gave her ibuprofen and got her as comfortable as possible. I elevated her feet, positioned my pack under her head, and placed her in the shade.

Since there was no cell phone reception and I couldn't hike her out on my own (it's about two miles of treacherous hiking and scrambling), I started running back to the trailhead for help around 12:30 p.m. I kept checking my phone for reception, and around 12:40 p.m. I was able to call 911 for a rescue team. I made it to the parking lot by 12:45 p.m. and waited a few more minutes for the paramedics to arrive. One of the paramedics and I hiked back in, reaching my partner around 1:30 p.m. A few minutes later, additional rescuers arrived with a

Stokes litter. Once she was stabilized in the litter, we started the carry out. It took roughly 30 people four hours to complete the evacuation.

She finally arrived at the hospital around 6:30 p.m. She underwent surgery for a tibia/fibula fracture (right leg) and a fibula fracture (left leg). She is expected to make a full recovery.

Analysis
Know the route, be aware of certain "no fall zones," and be extra careful in those areas. Also take extra precautions when routes have X or R ratings, and have the skills to initiate a self-rescue. (Source: Ryan Little.)

RAPPEL ERROR – ROPE IMPROPERLY THREADED THROUGH RAPPEL DEVICE, NO KNOT ON END OF ROPE
Hanging Rock State Park, Moores Wall
On July 8, Eric Metcalf (19), Ian Rogers (19), Addison Guranious (25), and Mitchell Martishius (23) began bouldering around 11 a.m. They planned to finish the day by rappelling Sentinel Buttress, a prominent 200-foot feature near the central part of the cliff. Starting at the base, the four scrambled to the top of the cliff and walked to the observation tower on Moores Knob, where they placed a number of cell phone calls. From here their plan was to rappel from the top of Sentinel Buttress to a ledge called the Crow's Nest, approximately halfway down the feature.

According to Addison, Mitchell was going to be the first to rappel. However, it was decided that Eric would descend first, since he was the most experienced and familiar with the terrain. Eric set up the rappel, and during the process Mitchell noted that one rope end hit the Crow's Nest rappel station below. He also noted that he and Eric had talked about tying a knot in the end of the rope, but did not remember Eric pulling up the rope to do this.

Eric rappelled out of sight from the other three. According to group members, Eric used the "two bolts at the top with the chain," which was a "solid anchor" and that it "looked safe." After Eric started to rappel, Mitchell heard the rope zipping, then observed the end of the rope as it ran through the anchor. The three then heard a loud thud. Mitchell leaned over the ledge and saw Eric lying face down on the Crow's Nest Ledge below, heard him moan, then roll over twice. The second roll sent him over the edge. All three heard a second thud as Eric landed at the base of the Sentinel Buttress almost 200 feet below.

All three made their way back to the Moores Knob observation tower to call 911. Ian descended to Eric. Addison and Mitchell hiked the Moores Wall Loop Trail to the campground, where they called 911 a second time. They waited there until picked up by a Hanging Rock State Park ranger.

In the meantime, Ian reached Eric, checked his pulse, felt a heartbeat, and began chest compressions, heard a crunching sound, stopped briefly, and continued compressions for approximately 10 minutes, then checked for a pulse. He then attempted rescue breathing but had trouble getting the breaths in, commenting that Eric's lungs were full of blood. He stopped CPR and ran down the trail to meet responding state park rangers. Both rangers attempted CPR and were unsuccessful. Paramedics arrived, and use of a defibrillator indicated no heart activity. Eric was pronounced dead on the scene. (Source: Hanging Rock State Park.)

Analysis

The Sentinel Buttress rappel anchor is located close to where the Sentinel Buttress route (5.5) finishes. The anchor, consisting of two bolts with hangers, swaged cable, and quick-links, is located just below the edge of a large, flat ledge. It is relatively easy to reach to the anchor, clip in, and then step down onto a small stance beside the anchor.

The rappel is normally done with a 60-meter rope. From this stance, one rappels approximately 30 meters (98.4 feet) to the Crow's Nest Ledge. This rappel starts as free-hanging, but quickly becomes less than vertical, eventually descending over large ledges. When rappelling with a short rope, one has to downclimb some low-angle, fourth-class terrain to reach Crow's Nest Ledge.

Once reaching the Crow's Nest Ledge, the climber makes his way about 15 feet north toward Sentinel Chimney and the top of the first pitch of Sentinel Buttress. Here one finds a fixed anchor of static rope wrapped around a large boulder, with rappel rings. From here it is about 85 feet to the ground.

Rescuers found a 50-meter rope attached to Eric's harness and lying completely on the ground when they arrived. Upon inspection, it was noted that a single bight of rope was threaded through the Black Diamond ATC Pro, which in turn was attached to a locking carabiner connected to the harness belay/rappel loop. The rope was measured from where the bight ran through the ATC. One side measured 95 feet, and the other 70 feet 6 inches. A figure-of-eight knot was tied approximately 6 feet 6 inches from the end of the shorter section of rope. No knot was observed on the 95-foot length of rope.

Based on this evidence and comments by Mitchell, it was determined that Eric rigged the rappel by running the 50-meter rope through the quick-links. He tied a figure-of-eight knot on one end of the rope, but did not place a blocking knot at the opposite end. When attaching the rappel rope to his harness, Eric neglected to thread both bights of rope through the ATC, as is required for a double-rope rappel. Instead, he placed a single bight of rope through his ATC and attached this to his harness. This proved to be a fatal mistake.

In the 2012 addition of *ANAM*, the opening section "Know the Ropes" provides instruction for rappelling. To repeat some of this: Before descending, do a pre-rappel check by having you and your partner(s) check the anchor and check the ropes to be sure they reach their intended destination, are even, and have blocking knots on both ends. Check the rappel device to make sure it is set up and oriented correctly; check the carabiner gate (locked); and assess the need for a backup. Eric was the only experienced climber in the group, therefore everyone else deferred to him for decisions regarding the rappel. (Source: Aram Attarian.)

FALL ON ROCK, CLIMBING ALONE
Pilot Mountain State Park

On July 30, Lloyd Ramsey (70), a local climber well known to the park staff and climbing community, was found dead at the base of the Foreign Trade Zone/Bat Out of Hell area. He had fallen a distance estimated at 50 feet by authorities. He was wearing his harness with a rope attached. No anchors were rigged for either a rappel or climb. Local climbers noted that Lloyd avoided rappelling, and he was also known to do a lot of roped solo climbing. Lloyd was careful about building anchors, but could be too casual around cliff edges. He suffered extensive trauma in the fall.

Analysis

State park rangers found Lloyd during the conduct of a hasty search after his van was found in the parking lot when the park had closed. He was wearing a climbing harness and hiking boots. His climbing pack was found at the top of the cliff, zipped shut and neatly organized. It contained his climbing shoes, some climbing gear, and water.

A 70-foot climbing rope was attached to his harness with a Grigri. Tied above the Grigri on the climbing rope was a double-loop figure-of-eight knot. The rope was attached to a doubled 50-foot rope (25 feet in length) that appeared to be prepared for an anchor with a locking carabiner and a double-loop figure-of-eight knot. The opposite end of the 25-foot anchor line had a double overhand loop tied into it. It was not attached to any anchor point. The investigation by state park personnel and experienced climbers was unable to identify a specific cause for this tragic incident. Climbing alone has many drawbacks. This is one of them. (Source: Pilot Mountain State Park, Aram Attarian.)

OREGON

FALL ON SNOW, UNABLE TO SELF-ARREST, FAULTY USE OF CRAMPONS – FAILED TO PUT THEM ON
Mt. Hood, South Side Route

On February 4, while ascending the South Side Route, Andy Kim (age unknown) stopped at the 9,500-foot elevation to put on his crampons. As he was leveling a platform for the transition, he slipped and slid about 500 feet. He lost his ice axe while attempting self-arrest. Joe Owens, a guide and mountain rescue leader, witnessed the fall and attended to Kim, who had suffered a forehead wound (and broken helmet) and sore limbs. Owens escorted Kim by short rope to a Timberline snowcat for ski patrol evacuation.

Analysis

Kim delayed donning crampons needed for purchase on the frozen snow surface. These conditions also made self-arrest problematic. (Source: Jeff Scheetz, Portland Mountain Rescue.)

FALL ON SNOW, UNABLE TO SELF-ARREST, PARTY SEPARATED
Mt. Hood, South Side Route

On February 5, while ascending the South Side Route, Meg Coker (35) lost her footing at about 10,500-foot elevation. She was unable to self-arrest and slid about 200 feet. She suffered multiple rib fractures and a collapsed lung. Nearby teams (not her teammates) witnessed the fall and provided first aid until professional ski patrollers and paramedics were on scene. A litter team from Portland Mountain Rescue provided sled evacuation to a Timberline snowcat.

Analysis

Coker fell behind her teammates, who were therefore not positioned to assist her. Climbing party strength is reduced when the team is separated. (Source: Jeff Scheetz, Portland Mountain Rescue.)

FALL ON SNOW – ICE AXE AND HELMET IN PACK
Mt. Hood, South Side Route

This fatal accident on February 6 was not witnessed, so many details remain unknown. Jared Townsley (31) was reported overdue from a solo climb on the South Side Route. He was last seen by other climbers descending near Crater Rock. A search team from Portland Mountain Rescue located his body on the upper White River Glacier (9,320-foot elevation) the next day. From the body position and a slide path, it appears Townsley suffered a long fall down the headwall of the White River Glacier. He succumbed to a catastrophic head injury.

Analysis

Weather conditions were reported favorable, and the climbing surface was typical melt/freeze crust. It is not known what triggered the fall. A successful self-arrest may have prevented the accident, but Townsley's ice axe was stowed on his backpack. A helmet may have limited the head injury, but his helmet also was stowed inside his pack. Crampons were found in the debris field, but it is not known if they were worn just prior to the accident. For some unknown reason, Townsley relaxed his vigilance during the descent and failed to benefit from the safety equipment that he carried in his pack. (Source: Bob Alexander, Portland Mountain Rescue.)

FALL ON SNOW, POSSIBLE FALLING ICE
Mt. Hood, South Side Route

On June 12, Mark Cartier (56), a highly experienced climber, succumbed after falling approximately 1,000 feet while soloing a South Side route variation. Climbing conditions were considered excellent.

Cartier suffered massive head trauma and was determined deceased on scene. His fall was not witnessed, so it is not known if icefall may have struck him and caused the fall. When an eight-person team from Portland Mountain Rescue recovered his remains, they noted substantial icefall by late morning.

Analysis

Solo climbing adds considerable risk and should only be conducted by confident and experienced climbers. In this case, climbing solo did not appear to cause or contribute to the accident.

Icefall can be a significant hazard, particularly for late ascents/descents. This accident happened at 5 a.m., well before substantial icefall was expected. By definition, experience level (both negative and positive) increases with the number of climbs, but so does the cumulative effect of risk. Perhaps the exposure of over 100 ascents finally caught up with this experienced climber. (Source: Bob Alexander, Portland Mountain Rescue.)

FALL ON SNOW, INADEQUATE EQUIPMENT, EXCEEDING ABILITIES
Mt. Hood, West Crater Rim

Gary Morgan (52) had flown in from Michigan and was attempting a summit climb on June 21 by a South Side variation, the West Crater Rim. After losing his footing, he was unable to self-arrest with his hiking stick. The 300-foot slide resulted in a concussion and hip/leg injuries. Nearby climbers (including Portland Mountain Rescue leaders Joe Owens, Michael Lemming, and Jarod Cogswell) witnessed the fall and provided first aid. Morgan was sled-evacuated by a PMR team to an awaiting Timberline snowcat.

Analysis

Morgan was observed to be under-equipped and demonstrated poor crampon technique when traversing to the "old chute." He lacked the ice axe and rigid mountaineering boots required for this route. His inexperience also prevented him from using from proper crampon technique. When asked about an ice axe, he responded "Nah, I travel light." (Source: Jeff Scheetz, Portland Mountain Rescue.)

FAILURE TO FOLLOW ROUTE, STRANDED, WEATHER
Mt. Hood, South Side Route

On November 28, Jeff Kish (30) soloed the South Side Route but was overcome by a storm during his descent. Unable to navigate in whiteout conditions at 10,600 feet, he called 911 on his cell phone and requested assistance. Despite the low visibility and high winds, rescuers from Portland Mountain Rescue reached him about 10 hours later. During this delay he placed numerous calls to friends, even texting a message to a Facebook page. Later communication attempts by SAR managers to facilitate Kish's rescue failed because of his dead cell phone battery.

Analysis

Climbers should not rely solely on cell phones to initiate a rescue. In this event, the cell phone (and automatic GPS data transmitted, via E911) was instrumental in rescuing Kish successfully.

Climbers using cell phones for emergencies should limit calls and conserve battery life. This may include placing/answering only critical calls, following instructions from SAR managers, following a predetermined call-back schedule, and leaving the phone turned off in between calls to save the battery. Phones also need to be kept warm and dry to maximize battery and display performance. (Source: Jeff Scheetz, Portland Mountain Rescue.)

(Editor's note: In June 2012, the Oregonian and OregonLive.com published a list of all fatalities on Mt. Hood since 1848, including ages and circumstances. About 10,000 people attempt to climb the mountain each year. The majority of rescues are for snowboarders, skiers, and hikers, with only about 4 percent for climbers.)

TENNESSEE

FALL ON ROCK, INADEQUATE PROTECTION – BOULDER DISLODGED
Prentice Cooper State Forest, Tennessee Wall

On February 10, a pair of experienced climbers were climbing Prerequisite for Excellence (5.8). The leader took a fall on a cam that was placed behind a block, dislodging the block (estimated to weigh approximately 200 pounds), which fell and hit his belayer, crushing his torso. According to a witness involved in the rescue, the belayer caught the fall on his Grigri, and was actually pulled up and into the falling boulder. She said that the belayer was wearing a helmet.

The belayer suffered a broken arm, ruptured spleen, and a "destroyed" knee. In spite of these injuries, he still managed to safely lower his climber after the fall. (Source: From a series of posts on Rockclimbing.com, February 13, 2012.)

Analysis

Placing gear in or behind blocks that may be loose is not recommended, since the camming or wedging action created by the unit can cause the block to shift or fall. This can be compounded by falling on the protection, as was the case in this situation. (Source: Aram Attarian.)

UTAH

FALL ON ROCK – RAPPEL ERROR
Big Cottonwood Canyon, Challenge Buttress

On September 20, according to Unified Police Capt. Kris Ownby, two men (23 and 31) were rappelling down the Challenge Buttress, just across from Storm Mountain, about 8 p.m. One of them fell off the end of the rope, and both fell as a result because they were simul-rappelling. One fell 10 feet, and the other fell 40 feet. Ownby said the 23-year-old suffered a lower leg laceration and a possible sprained ankle, but his companion sustained more severe injuries to his legs and upper body.

About 20 rescuers, including four paramedics, responded to the scene. The 23-year-old climber was aided in completing his ascent by 9:30 p.m. and drove himself to a hospital to be checked out. The other climber was lowered by rescuers shortly thereafter and taken to University Hospital in serious but non-life-threatening condition. (Source: Edited from an article by Bob Mims in *The Salt Lake Tribune*.)

Analysis

I was the 23-year-old involved in the accident. We are still not sure what happened. My friend and I were still hooked onto the rope after we fell because I had knotted the ends. All I remember is him falling really fast and hitting the ground, and then I fell as a result. I have simul-rappelled several times before. I still do not know what went wrong or what I should do differently in the future. I do think I need to start using prusiks for backup, especially when using single ropes.

My friend is doing OK. He has a fractured vertebrae, but the doctors say he will heal up 100 percent.

FALL ON ROCK, INADEQUATE PROTECTION
Fisher Towers, Ancient Art Tower

On April 25 a woman (25) fell 20 feet, landing on a ledge about 200 feet up from the base of the tower. She suffered rib, spine, and head injuries, and was flown by Life Flight Helicopter to Intermountain Healthcare in Murray, Utah. According to the Grand County Sheriff's Office, the woman slipped and fell while trying to clip into a bolt. (Source: Veronica Harvery.)

FALL ON ROCK, RAPPEL ERROR – ROPES UNEVEN
No Man's Canyon

It was with special interest that I obtained the 2012 edition of *Accidents in North American Mountaineering*, because the "Know the Ropes" section focuses on rappelling. My brother, Louis Cicotello (70), did not survive a fall while on rappel at the exit of the North Fork of No Man's Canyon, a slot canyon in southeastern Utah, on March 6, 2011. As a result of his fall, I was stranded for six days on a ledge until rescued by Wayne County SAR.

That day we carried only one rope that was 60 meters (200 feet) long. I have every confidence that Louis checked the midpoint of that rope, which was always marked with a piece of white tape (either climber's or first-aid tape), and that he coiled it correctly at home as he made preparations for our trip. The rope was in the truck until he packed it in his bag that morning. We had warmed up the day before in a nearby canyon, but used a shorter rope to complete the rappels.

We had pulled that rope through four different rappels in No Man's Canyon prior to the set-up of the second stage of the exit rappel (the 100-foot section).

Louis set up each rappel and I assisted. Each time we watched for the tape mark. Each time Louis went first on rappel. The first three rappels in the canyon were short, each one in the 25- to 30-foot range. There was no issue of having plenty of length for both strands of the rope on each of those rappels. In fact, one of the descents was described in the guide as a "downclimb," but Louis took precaution to use the rope and set up a rappel. He remarked, "After all, I am 70 years old."

The exit rappel had two stages. The first was in the 40- to 50-foot range, and the rappeller had a view from the pour-off launch point to the landing area below. The surplus length of each strand was clearly visible once the rope was tossed down.

The second stage of the exit rappel was set up from a bolt and hanger on the canyon wall near the top of a narrow crevice. The crevice sloped like a sliding board, with only enough space between the canyon walls to allow one person to go down at a time. The crevice was nearly 20 feet from the top to the bottom, where it met the edge of the canyon wall. The sling that Louis and I set up was 10 to 12 feet long, so that the rappel ring would lie beyond a groove in the middle of the slope to avoid any possibility that the rope would get stuck when pulled from below. At the bottom of that crevice, near the edge, was enough space for the rappeller to stand (if he wished) before beginning the descent.

Louis went down first. He tied into the sling near the anchor, backing down the crevice. He did not stop and stand at the edge before beginning his descent. As he was maneuvering himself over the edge, he told me to be careful not to get my hands pinched between the rope and the lip of the rock face. Once over the edge, Louis told me that he was on the free portion of the rappel. He was out of my sight as soon as he went over the edge. A few seconds later, Louis called up to me that he could see that the ropes were unequal but that it was "no biggie." Those were his last words. Almost immediately, the rope whipped through the rappel ring and disappeared below.

Analysis

The fall was not related to any failure of equipment. It was a case of uneven ropes that was tragically discovered too late. Louis was an experienced climber and had summited many of the fourteeners in Colorado. I was a latecomer to climbing, having begun in 2006. The two of us planned and completed annual weeklong trips through many technical canyons in Utah.

What happened to make those strands unequal? In all the set-ups in which that rope was used before and during that canyon trip, Louis always looked for that piece of tape as the center point. The rope had a darkish, stained section in the middle of it. Louis used a piece of first aid or climbing tape as a visible marker in the center of that stained section. It was not always firmly attached to the rope, and he repeatedly vowed to "fix" the position of the tape more securely as a future project when he was at home.

That tape marker started out in the middle of the rope. Whether it gradually moved each time the rope was pulled through the rings/quick-links on the previous rappels, or whether the majority of the slippage occurred on the first stage of the exit rappel, I can't say for certain. As we threaded the rope for the second stage of the exit rappel, we watched for that piece of tape on the rope, and when it came near the rappel ring, we stopped threading. We based everything we did from that point on what we thought was the middle of the rope.

At that juncture, the rope strands were tossed down the crevice and over the edge. As a result, there was no tying the ends of the strands into a knot.

One afternoon, after returning to Colorado Springs, a family friend and I laid that rope out to check its length. The 60-meter rope laid out nearly 200 feet, so it was long enough when double-stranded through the rappel device to complete a 100-foot rappel. What we noticed was the tape was nowhere near the center of the rope. It was approximately 10 feet from one end.

(Editor's note: This accident was not reported to us for the 2012 edition. We are grateful to David Cicotello for sending it to us this year. It is worthy of inclusion because of the issue of the use of tape for marking the center of a rope. Holding the ends of a rappel rope and coiling it until coming to the center, combined with knotting the ends with stopper knots, are both recommended.)

RAPPEL ERROR – TANGLED IN ROPES, INEXPERIENCED
Zion National Park, Subway

On September 18, Yoshio Hosobuchi (74), a retired neurosurgeon, was found dead after spending a night hanging upside down on his climbing ropes. He had been making a rappel in the Subway, a popular and demanding canyoneering route.

Hosobuchi was from Novato, California, and had no experience navigating the Subway. He was caught about midway in a narrow, nine-mile chasm with fast-moving cold water. His wife (61) was unable to free her husband, who was found hanging over a waterfall, said Superintendent Jock Whitworth. She hiked out after some difficulty to alert rangers, who had to wait until early the next day to recover his body with a helicopter.

Analysis

The couple had received local training on navigating slot canyons and had successfully climbed Keyhole Canyon on the park's east side before taking their "bucket list" trip into the Subway.

Park authorities said that when Hosobuchi's rope jammed in his belay device, he used a knife to cut his waist belt in an effort to free himself. However, the harness slipped down his legs and became entangled with his right foot as he tumbled over headfirst inside the waterfall. Hosobuchi appeared to be pinned by the force of rushing water, said park spokeswoman Alyssa Baltrus. This was the first death of a hiker/climber in the Subway in many years. What is known is that the man bypassed a more gentle descent down a rock slab for a vertical descent that left him unable to use his feet to maintain traction with rock.

Hanging in a harness for too long, especially upside down, can cut off a climber's blood circulation, said Mike Banach, a guide with Zion Mountain School who is familiar with the Subway. He said many climbers are left at their own peril because commercial guiding is prohibited inside the park. "People are going in without knowledge or experience, and don't even have the ability to hire a guide," said Banach. The accident happened at a 30-foot drop that isn't considered difficult if done correctly.

Park Superintendent Whitworth said of the Subway: "It is a very popular trail, but very difficult—the nine-mile hike requires rappelling and ascending skills, extensive routefinding experience, and swimming through several cold and deep pools. Unfortunately, its location inside the wilderness also means that rescues are not always possible or timely enough. Sound decision-making and problem-solving are critical."

"Our message is you can learn the basics of canyoneering, but what happens when something goes wrong is hard to teach quickly," said Baltrus. (Source: Edited from an article by Paul Foy, Associated Press.)

(Editor's note: Two articles on the subject of hanging in a harness are recommended by Dr. Joe Forrester: Mortimer, RB, Risks and Management of Prolonged Suspension in an Alpine Harness, WEMJ 2011 (22) 77-86; and Pasquier, et al, Clinical Update: Suspension Trauma, WEMJ 2011 (22) 167-171.)

FALL ON ROCK, PROTECTION PULLED OUT
Zion National Park

On October, 26 Lyle Dale Hurd III (49) died after taking a fall while climbing the Northeast Buttress, a popular route on Angels Landing. Hurd was in a party of four individuals, traveling in pairs; Hurd and his partner were following the other pair up the route. Hurd was leading the fifth pitch when he fell over 40 feet onto a ledge, after pulling out his top piece of protection. His partner witnessed the fall and called 911 before providing medical care to Hurd. Twenty members of the Zion Search and Rescue Team responded. When park medics reached the ledge, they confirmed that Hurd had not survived his injuries. The SAR team worked through the night to evacuate the body and investigate the fall.

Analysis

The Northeast Buttress is an eight-pitch climb that is rated IV 5.10+. This was Hurd's first time climbing this particular route, although he was an experienced climber and had completed several big-wall climbs previously in Zion National Park. This was the second fatal accident in the park for 2012, and the seventh climbing fatality since 1983. (Source: Edited from a news release by Zion National Park spokeswoman Alyssa Baltrus.)

VIRGINIA

FALL ON ROCK
Shenandoah National Park, Old Rag Mountain

On March 31, Art Webb (51) was climbing the Piton Crack (5.7) on Skyline Wall when he took a short pendulum fall (under 10 feet) on a traversing tight-hand and finger crack. The fall caused him to strike a chunk of rock on a small, jutting arête, breaking his leg just above the ankle. Due to the late hour, and after discussion with medical control, the decision was made for EMS/SAR personnel to spend the night on Old Rag with the victim. A U.S. Park Police air rescue helicopter conducted a litter-hoist evacuation the next day.

Analysis

This was truly a freak occurrence. It is unlikey that the accident could be reproduced. Just poor luck. (Source: Aram Attarian.)

FALL ON ROCK, PROTECTION PULLED, NO HELMET
Great Falls

On September 9, Dennis (27) and TJ (25) were trad climbing Armbuster (5.9), located in the Bird's Nest area of Great Falls. Leading the route, TJ fell at the crux a few feet above his top piece of protection. This top piece, a nut that had held previous leader falls, popped out, and another nut and a cam placed within one and a half body lengths of the top piece also pulled out. The next piece was too low on the route to prevent TJ from falling approximately 20 feet to the ground.

A first responder noted, "I ran over and found a male climber sitting at the base of the climb with a little blood on the front of his shirt. I asked if he was OK, and he told me that he hit the back of his head. He knew his name, where he was, and what day it was. I looked at the helmet sitting next to him and said, 'Luckily you had your helmet on.' His reply, 'I didn't.' Upon further examination, I noted a large laceration on the back of his head, with blood streaming down his back." Injuries included a laceration to the head, concussion, and a fractured foot.

Analysis

The rock in this area has a reputation for failing or allowing protection to slip out. We won't trad climb on this rock again. Additionally, our rope was well-used (1.5 years old, I believe). It was stiff, and we didn't change ends or retie knots between falls. The condition of the rope, combined with a relatively static belay, probably exerted more force on the protection than was necessary. And always wear a helmet. (Source: Dennis—last name unknown—and M. Brown.)

WASHINGTON

FALL ON SNOW, NO HELMET
North Cascades, Luna Peak, Access Creek Basin

On July 14, Stan Boyle (50), Juan Lira (58), Tim Browning (52), Craig Rankine (55), Kevin Weed (49), and I (Chris Robertson, 57) took a Ross Lake Resort Boat to the Big Beaver Camp, landing at about 12:30 p.m. We hiked to Luna Camp in intermittent light rain, where we met Bill Davis (50) and Walt Boserberg (50), members of an independent climbing party.

After hiking for two days, on Monday we continued into the Access Creek Basin. We started up the gully that leads to a col at about 6,000 feet on the Southeast Ridge of Luna Peak. The route consists of a lower gully that is about 25 to 30 feet wide at its narrowest. About 800 feet above the basin floor, the snow ended in mixed talus, soil, and heather. On the climber's right side of the gully, the soil and talus was 35 degrees. Above the rocks, the average snow slopes were between 30 and 42 degrees. Down low, the snow was firm and good for step kicking, but higher up the snow was harder.

Between 11:15 and 11:30 a.m., the group began arriving at the col. Craig arrived next to last, with Kevin a short distance behind. Bill Davis reported, "At about 11:45 a.m., I heard a cry and looked down to see Kevin (just feet from the top) slip from a step. I expected to see a quick self-arrest. Kevin had his axe in his upper hand and a ski pole in his lower hand. After three to five seconds, he was sliding on his chest very fast, and there did not seem to be a break in his speed at all.... After he had slid about 300 to 400 vertical feet, I believe he lost his pole and certainly his axe. Any attempt to arrest was gone. Shortly after, he began to tumble and I lost [sight of] him as the couloir turned a bit." (We estimate the slopes were between 35 and 38 degrees in the narrow portions where Kevin slid.)

We began organizing immediately. I asked Juan to look for Kevin with binoculars. Tim began descending to provide immediate assistance. Bill stood by with a SPOT device to be used if needed.

Tim said, "I started noticing Kevin's equipment several hundred feet from the top of the ridge."

I descended and caught up to Tim about 800 feet below the col. As we approached the rocks below the col, we still could not see Kevin. I asked Tim to stand by so he could signal to the group at the col and began descending the lower gully.

I found Kevin at about 4,800 feet on the climber's left side of the gully, mostly on soil and rock. His feet were below him and he was prone. I immediately noticed large lacerations on his head, with a 1.5-by-2-inch skin flap. He responded weakly but was not completely aware of where he was or what had occurred. I shouted up to Tim to signal the group above that Kevin was alive and would require a helicopter evacuation. Because of the distance, communication was difficult. Bill activated the SPOT at noon after attempts to use the cell phone failed.

Kevin did not have severe bleeding. He believed he had broken his clavicle and humerus. He had a laceration in his right triceps as well as other superficial abrasions. I cut his pack off and removed his boots.

After confirming that the SPOT had been activated, Tim came down to assist. We could not find Kevin's sleeping pad, so we placed the tent and then his sleeping bag on a less steep slope below him. Tim and I moved Kevin by sliding him along the length of his body to reduce movement to his back and neck. We were not able to get Kevin completely onto the sleeping bag; we covered him with the remaining contents of his pack.

The rest of the group used ropes to belay the descent and to lower my pack and Tim's. They arrived shortly. With our full group, we placed Kevin completely in his sleeping bag. We then covered him with three additional sleeping bags. We excavated a platform with a snow shovel and moved Kevin there, lifting him uniformly with his sleeping bag. At this point, we also had two Thermarest pads under him. We heated enough water for four hot water bottles, which we placed near him.

Bill and Walt, the independent climbers, had agreed to stay at the col until the helicopter arrived. We were concerned if they continued on their route, the SPOT location would move and cause confusion. The National Park Service (NPS) helicopter arrived at 3:30 p.m. Initially, the helicopter personnel interpreted Bill and Walt's signals as, "We fell down the gully, but were now we are OK." After a few minutes, the NPS helicopter crew reportedly considered leaving, under the assumption that Bill and Walt were OK. However, they noted that every time they flew past, Bill and Walt's gestures became more adamant pointing downhill. Further, Bill and Walt had not pushed the "All OK" button on the SPOT. The helicopter crew checked and found two backcountry permits issued for the area (Bill and Walt, and our team of six); therefore they decided to expand the search toward Access Creek Basin.

At 3:35 p.m. they saw the flash from our signal mirror and located us in the gully. The helicopter flew down to the Access Creek Basin, setting down at 3:42. Once it was clear we were in communication with the helicopter, Bill and Walt left (around 4 p.m.). [*Rescuer note: We flew to the SPOT coordinates. The SPOT was being held by an uninjured, bystander party. It did not actually take us a long time to figure out where the injured party was. The uninjured bystanders who owned the SPOT, and whom we first located, largely emphasized and mouthed to us, "We are OK." This did at first lead us to think that the call was unfounded or resolved, and that we could fly away. Simply pointing in the direction of the injured/involved climbers and still looking like you need assistance would be recommended for cases where an uninjured/uninvolved party uses their SPOT for someone else.*]

I descended to the helicopter and met and briefed Kelly Bush (wilderness district ranger), Kevork Arackellion (lead climbing ranger), and Jason Moorhead (pilot for HiLine Helicopters). They conferred and decided to insert Kevork by short-hauling with the NPS helicopter, and then bring in a backboard and litter, and short-haul Kevin to the basin. They called Airlift Northwest to evacuate Kevin from the basin. By 4:30 p.m., Kevork was at the accident site; Kevin was short-hauled at 5:17; and by 5:30 Airlift Northwest had flown out with Kevin, taking him to Harborview Hospital in Seattle.

He received 30 stitches to his scalp, and his triceps wound was closed. Kevin also had a shattered and dislocated shoulder/humerus bone, fractured eye socket, and fractured cheekbone. A nerve in his shoulder was severely and potentially permanently damaged. Kevin went into surgery July 17 and emerged with a new plate on his humerus that has 13 screws. On July 20, Kevin was moved to the rehabilitation center, and he was discharged to home on July 28. By October, Kevin had limited strength in his right arm, had limited feeling in his right forearm and hand, and still had problems isolating conversations in large groups. He is optimistic about his future and expects to climb, compete in triathlons, and ski.

Analysis

Lessons learned:

• We all should have been wearing helmets anywhere falling or rockfall was a possibility.

• The SPOT device allowed us to get Kevin to medical attention within about seven hours of the accident and saved an overnight bivouac. We had no cellular phone reception on the ridge, so a cell phone was useless.

• The SPOT device allowed us to get Kevin to medical attention within about seven hours of the accident and saved an overnight bivouac.

• We had no cellular phone reception on the ridge, so a cell phone was useless.

• Because we registered our party, the NPS knew we were in the area. Had we not done so, they may have flown away once they saw that Bill and Walt were OK.

• Everyone in a party should have a copy of other party members' emergency contact information.

• An accident report form would have been helpful to prompt us to record appropriate information, which is easily forgotten during an emergency response. This would have been more important if we had to hike out for help.

• Before splitting the party to respond to an emergency, take a few minutes to plan, and agree on communication protocols and contingency actions.

• Keep the entire party engaged and encourage ideas. For example, Craig recognized the need to signal the helicopter and suggested using a signal mirror.

• Everyone in the party should carry a compass that has a good signal mirror and should practice using it. (Few in our party knew how to signal with a mirror.) The pilot reported that he might not have found us had he not seen the flash from our signal mirror.

• When traveling in steep conditions, wear long pants and long-sleeve shirts, as this can help to prevent or reduce scrapes and lacerations from lesser falls.

• Rescue/reconnaissance helicopters should be equipped with a bullhorn or other means to communicate with people on the ground. One possibility would be having inexpensive Family Radio Service (FRS) radios that could be dropped or lowered.

(Source: Edited from a long report prepared by Chris Robertson. Tim Browning, Juan Lira, Craig Rankine, and Walt Davis prepared independent accounts, which weare incorporated in this report.)

FALL INTO CREVASSE, PROTECTION PULLED OUT
North Cascades, Ruth Mountain

On September 9 a party of three male climbers had already summited Ruth Mountain at 7:45 a.m. On the way down, Anthony Fiorillo, who described himself as an experienced climber, offered to give some lessons in crevasse rescue to his two climbing buddies, Keith LeMay and Jefferson Morriss. Morriss was below in the crevasse, while LeMay and Fiorillo were on top of the crevasse. All three climbers were attached to a single picket. The picket failed, and all three fell to the bottom of the crevasse. They were wearing crampons and injured each other as they fell. The least injured of the three was able to climb out of the crevasse, but brought no rope or anchors with him.

A separate party of three happened upon the scene and found Fiorillo atop the crevasse, waiting for rescue. He had used a cell phone to call 911. It is somewhat surprising that cell service was available at this location. This very experienced party, which included a mountain guide who is also the author of a guidebook for the Cascades, set up two individual anchors away from the lip (buried T-slot ice axes with girth-hitched runners on them). This proved to be a better anchor, given the snow conditions on that day. One climber rappelled to the injured climbers in the crevasse on a separate rope and attached a loop of rope into the carabiners on their harnesses. The two bystander rescuers pulled them out one at a time using a straight C-pulley with a Tibloc (Petzl ascending device) up top to keep from losing ground when pulling. They were able to pull them out in a few minutes.

The NPS rescue team arrived by helicopter, deploying one ranger by a toe-in "landing" at the scene, and another ranger at a staging site at the base of the glacier. With the help of the on-scene climbers, the two seriously injured and hypothermic patients were short-hauled to the staging site. Two separate Airlift Northwest medical helicopters arrived and transported the patients to hospitals. The third climber was evacuated to the trailhead by the NPS helicopter and transported for minor medical needs. LeMay suffered broken ribs, and Morriss had a large gash on his head.

Analysis

Several review points are obvious from this incident. The injured climbing party was quite fortunate that the bystander climbers happened into the scene. (NPS rescuers also felt fortunate for this, as it would have been a more difficult rescue, later, with more critical patients had they not.) That the climbing party was practicing crevasse rescue is a good thing. (Many climbers do not follow through with this after first learning glacier travel, ice axe use, etc.). The obvious root cause of this incident stemmed from using a single anchor for all members of the party. It was observed by the rangers that the placement of the dead-man anchor was shallow (it was unclear whether it was a picket or an ice axe that had been used), and it did not appear that a slot had been dug in the snow for the runner to exit the snow in line with the angle of pull. (Source: Edited from reports by Caleb Hutton in *The Bellingham Herald* on September 10, 2012, and Kelly Bush, Wilderness District Ranger, North Cascades National Park.)

FALL ON SNOW, FALL INTO CREVASSE
Mt. Rainer, Emmons Glacier

On June 21 climbing rangers and an independent climber at Camp Schurman, Claire Kuhgen, witnessed an accident that involved a team of four climbers (two males, 51 and 31, and two females, 18 and 22) from Waco, Texas. The four climbers, Stuart Smith, Ross VanDyke, Noel Smith, and Stacy Wren, were roped together and fell down the mountain after a successful summit attempt, sliding out of control. Two members fell into a crevasse and stopped the rope team from tumbling further. Two climbing rangers, Jeremy Shank and Peter Ellis, were dispatched by climbing ranger David Gottlieb, who assumed the role of incident commander. Shank and Ellis left from Camp Schurman around noon toward the scene.

At 12:43 p.m., park dispatch received a 911 call from Ross VanDyke, reporting a climbing accident on the Emmons Glacier. He reported there were four people involved: one was "bouncing," one was in a crevasse, one had two possible broken legs, and the caller reported that he might also have a broken leg. He stated that everyone was bloody, but conscious. All were roped together. Dispatch told VanDyke that a ground team should arrive at his location around 2 p.m., and that a helicopter was on its way as well. Climbing ranger Gottlieb, who was stationed at White River, immediately requested helicopter support from Joint Base Lewis-McChord (JBLM) for the rescue effort.

An incident command post (ICP) was set up at the Emergency Operations Center in Longmire, starting at 12:45 p.m. An Army Reserve Chinook helicopter, Hooker 213, was dispatched from JBLM at 1:47 p.m., and landed at Kautz Helibase at 2:06 with full crew and two military medics. At 2:51 it took off with four climbing rangers—Nick Hall, Jon Bowman, Joe Akers, and Cameron Reade—and Mil-Ops Rich Lechleitner on board, headed for the scene of the accident. Gottlieb passed on the role of incident command to climbing ranger Thomas Payne as soon as the ICP was set up in Longmire and the Hooker 213 had been ordered. Gottlieb remained as operations section chief. At 2:30 p.m., Payne dispatched climbing rangers Cooper Self and Will Tarantino to respond via a route up and over the mountain from Camp Muir to the accident scene at 13,800 feet on the Emmons Glacier.

Shank and Ellis arrived on scene around 2 p.m. and began extricating the climbers from the crevasse and making patient assessments. Shank reported that Stacy Wren (22) had hit her head and lost consciousness, but that she was OK. Noel Smith (18) was alert and oriented times four, had "a raspberry" on her forehead, and was experiencing abdominal and pelvic pain. The rangers also reported that the two men had broken legs, lacerations, and contusions related to the fall, and that one had point tenderness on his spine.

At 3:13 p.m., Hooker 213 hoisted climbing rangers Jon Bowman and Nick Hall (34) and rescue equipment to the scene. By 3:25, the patients were being stabilized, packaged, and prepared for hoisting. The initial plan was to hoist all four patients into Hooker 213 and transport them to Madigan. However, it was determined by Hall that two of the patients needed advanced life support (ALS) care, so Airlift Northwest was requested to fly to Sunrise to stage. An ALS ambulance was also requested to respond and stage at Sunrise. During this time, there were various radio communications that reported difficulty in communicating with the Mil-Ops. Eventually the rescuers determined that the best communication with the helicopter was using a line-of-sight, air-to-ground channel MORA Com-2. Hall decided to use that frequency at 4:20 p.m. At 4:30, Hall notified operations that they were ready for the hoist operation to begin. He stated that there was a clear plan in place, communications were good, and everyone was ready to go.

At 4:53 p.m., one patient was successfully hoisted onto the helicopter, but wind was hampering the lowering of the empty litter to get more patients. The empty litter was raised back into Hooker 213 and a tag line was attached. The tag line was then lowered out to Hall to help stabilize the litter. Hall reeled in the litter, and just after he unclipped the litter from the hoist, he began to slip. Bowman reported that Hall and the litter began sliding down the glacier at a high rate of speed. Bowman, Ellis, and Shank were still on the scene with three patients. Payne recognized the developing situation and requested additional support. Climbing rangers Glenn Kessler and Brian Hasebe were tasked with coordinating an aviation response to the second incident. Alpine district ranger Stefan Lofgren assumed incident command.

At 5:03 p.m., a second helicopter was requested from JBLM, but the rescuers were informed it would be three hours before a second helicopter would be available. At 5:04, the Hooker 213 was diverted to search for Hall. Hall was located three minutes later, at approximately 11,300 feet on the Winthrop Glacier. They reported the victim was not moving.

Operations directed Akers to get on scene with Hall to start providing care. Akers was inserted on the Winthrop Glacier via aft-landing at 10,900 feet. Hooker 213 reported that it was low on fuel and was heading to JBLM to refuel with Reade, Lechleitner, and one patient onboard. The patient was transported to Madigan Army Hospital once Hooker 213 got back to base to refuel.

At 5:09 p.m., a request was made to bring Airlift Northwest to Sunrise. Tarantino and Self were instructed to descend back to a solid landing zone for a possible hoist into Hall's location. At 5:24, Akers reported that he was approaching Hall. Ellis led the members of the climbing team that were near the accident scene back down to Camp Schurman.

At 5:37 p.m., Akers was on scene with Hall, and two minutes later he reported Hall was deceased. At 5:43, Airlift Northwest landed at Sunrise to stage. At 6:40 p.m., Northwest Helicopter dispatched a contract helicopter N900FF (OFF) to Kautz with an ETA of 30 minutes. At 6:54, Hooker 213 landed at Kautz. By 7:15 p.m., Hall was packaged in a litter and ready for evacuation. At 7:31, OFF landed at Kautz. At 7:45 p.m., Hooker 213 flew back to original accident scene to resume evacuation efforts for the remaining patients on the mountain. Two more patients were hoisted off. Only one patient, Stacy Wren, was left on scene. Hooker 213 was then redirected to evacuate Akers from Hall's location at 8:15 p.m., and Airlift Northwest reported they had to leave, as they were running out of daylight. At the end of the day, Bowman and Shank were camped out with the last patient for the night, and Self, Tarantino, and Ellis were at Camp Schurman.

On June 22 operations began to evacuate the last patient from the scene with Shank and Ellis, and to retrieve Hall's body from 11,300 feet on the Winthrop. At 6:30 a.m., Shank reported they were getting ready to depart the scene. At 7 a.m., Gottlieb met with the ground strike team of seven other rangers and left White River for Camp Schurman. At 7:05, Shank and Bowman left the accident scene at 13,700 feet and started their descent in whiteout conditions. By 8 a.m., Shank had requested Self and Tarantino to help assist him and Bowman with the patient. Self and Tarantino went from Camp Schurman to the top of the corridor to assist. Both the patient with the rangers and the ground strike team from White River arrived safely back at Camp Schurman around noon. Weather conditions weren't suitable for searching for Hall, and search operations were suspended for the rest of the day. Self, Ellis, Bowman, Tarantino, and Hutchins escorted the patient down from Camp Schurman to White River Ranger Station that afternoon, arriving around 5 p.m.

Ranger Hall's body was removed on July 5 after a period of poor weather. (Source: Daniel Camiccia, Wilderness Ranger.)

HYPOTHERMIA, UNDERESTIMATING PERSONAL FITNESS
Mt. Rainier

On July 16 an independent climbing party notified RMI guides that there was a climbing party on the summit requesting help. One of the members of the team had signs and symptoms of hypothermia, and they were hunkered down in a steam vent near the register rock on the summit. RMI guides notified NPS rangers at 8 a.m. At 11 a.m., NPS rangers Self and Reade responded from Camp Muir with two RMI guides. NPS aviation resources were placed on standby for a possible summit extraction.

As the ground team led by ranger Self was ascending, rangers at Camp Schurman reported that three members of the injured climber's party had descended to Camp Schurman. They reported that the team was composed of eight climbers, and that there were still five climbers on the summit, including the patient. The patient's chief complaint was "feeling cold." They said their team had reached the crater rim at the summit around 6 a.m., and that the patient wasn't feeling good even before the summit. They reported the patient had a productive cough with blood, trouble with bowel movements that morning, and a medical history that included a recently discovered tumor in his intestines.

They had left the summit at 8 a.m. to ask for help, and said the five members at the summit did not have a solid plan of what they were going to do. Before ranger Self's team reached the crater rim, the weather cleared and the Camp Schurman rangers reported a team of five was at 13,800 feet and moving slowly down toward Camp Schurman. Rangers Ellis and Shank climbed from Camp Schurman to meet the party on their descent. Ranger Self's team reached the summit at 2:45 p.m. and reported there was no one in any obvious steam cave location. Rangers Ellis and Shank met the party on the Emmons-Winthrop route at about 12,500 feet. They did a quick patient assessment and assisted the party back down to Camp Schurman starting at 4:30 p.m. All resources were safely out of the field by 7 p.m.

Analysis

A common misconception about Mt. Rainer is that the crater and steam caves surrounding the summit can offer relief from poor conditions. Though some temporary relief can be found, in general it is not a good idea to keep ascending to find shelter. It is also ill-advised to depend on these steam caves for shelter.

Descending to lower elevations—and preferably a high camp—is generally a much better decision. Thankfully, the party was able to warm and hydrate the patient and get him moving back down the hill, which was impressive. It is rare that teams are prepared enough to self-rescue. The party made a good decision to bring stoves and sleeping bags.

Additionally, the patient had a known current medical condition and had decided to continue toward the summit, disregarding his health. This put both him and his climbing partners in danger. Good physical health and fitness cannot be overemphasized as a safety matter. (Source: Daniel Camiccia, Wilderness Ranger.)

(*Editor's note: While not an accident, this near miss is worth inclusion because of its lessons.*)

FALL ON SNOW, PARTY SEPARATED – INEXPERIENCED LEADERSHIP
Mt. Rainier, Muir Snowfield

On July 21, Marc Shokeir (42) sustained injuries in a fall on Mt. Rainier. At 2:20 p.m., he made it down to Camp Muir, but was unable to get himself down from the high camp and requested assistance from rangers. A plan was made to have climbing rangers ski the injured climber to the bottom of the Muir Snowfield, where he would be transferred to a litter team that would take him the rest of the way to the Paradise parking lot. However, as resources were being assembled, a second call came in from an Alpine Ascents International guide, Sam Hannesy, reporting that Cody Corbett (16) had sustained a head injury when he slipped while hiking to Camp Muir. He was separated from his party at approximately 9,000 feet on the Muir Snowfield. Corbett had called his mother on his cell phone at about 2:30 p.m., reporting to her that he had hit his head on a rock and was delirious and concerned about himself.

All resources were diverted to the rescue of this patient, as it was felt to be the more critical situation. [*See next report for details about Shokeir's rescue.*] Park climbing ranger Nick Armitage and volunteer William Tarantino were contacted and responded from Camp Muir. They located Corbett at 8,900 feet, southwest of Moon Rocks and 200 yards northwest of the main trail route. Armitage provided medical care. Given his injury and physical condition, airlift operations were considered necessary to evacuate the patient. With help from two Rainier Mountaineering and two Alpine Ascent International guides, as well as climbing rangers Carrie Tomlinson and Jonathan Bowman, Corbett was carried down to Pebble Creek in a rescue sled. He was then carried by wheeled litter to Panorama Point by an additional SAR team. At Panorama Point, the patient was airlifted to Harborview Hospital.

Analysis

Cody Corbett had started hiking from the Paradise parking lot at 9:30 a.m. with 12 other people from the South Hill Calvary Chapel. Phil Spagnolo, associate pastor, was the leader, and Jimmie Caldwall was helping watch out for the group. Spagnolo stated that their plan was to hike to Camp Muir, and if someone decided to turn back, they would meet at the Paradise parking lot. It was Corbett's first time hiking to Camp Muir, and Spagnolo had just met the patient for the first time that morning.

At 11:45 a.m., on the Muir Snowfield, the group stopped for lunch and realized that Corbett was not with them. He had last been seen at 10:30 at the tail end of the group. The group continued to Camp Muir and returned to the parking lot at 4 p.m. Unable to find Corbett at the parking lot, Caldwall started searching back up the Camp Muir Trail. On the trail, Caldwall contacted ranger Jordan Mammel and other members of the rescue party, and was informed of the patient's condition and his transfer to Harborview.

Corbett was released from Harborview Hospital on July 22. He was diagnosed as having a concussion, a bruise above his left ear, and bruised ribs. He explained that when he was hiking with the group he stopped for a quick break, and he thought that the rest of the group had heard him saying he was stopping for a minute. When he looked up to continue, the group was gone. Determined to get to Camp Muir, he kept hiking uphill, but was not certain of the route. About two or three hours later, he slipped and hit his head on a boulder. He stated that after that he lost track of time and was confused. He did not remember calling his mom on his cell phone at 2:30 p.m. He does remember that some people had talked to him, and that he did make it to Camp Muir. Upon leaving Camp Muir, he was told that he was headed the wrong way, toward a dangerous cliff area. He had also suffered from a bad case of sunburn and occasional headaches, but was feeling better and expected a full recovery.

Analysis

When hiking or climbing in groups, it is important to ensure that all members of the group are accounted for. This is particularly true of groups of minors in the outdoors. Frequent stops with counts of all participants are necessary to ensure that no one is left behind. (Source: Daniel Camiccia, Wilderness Ranger.)

(Editor's note: This is not actually a climbing accident, but important to include because of the situation in which an inexperienced group gets into trouble because of not paying attention to basics, especially in potentially hazardous terrain.)

FALL ON SNOW
Mt. Rainer, Disappointment Cleaver

[See report above for the introduction to this incident.] On July 21 at noon, rangers Jon Bowman, Nick Armitage, and Will Tarantino were descending Disappointment Cleaver at 12,000 feet when they made contact with a party of four that appeared to be descending slowly. The party leader stated that one member of the team, Marc Shokeir (42), had taken a fall near the top of the Cleaver. He suffered an injury to his ribs, but was ambulatory. The party was offered assistance by Bowman, but the party leader declined, stating that they were moving slowly but would be able to descend to Camp Muir under their own power.

At 2 p.m., these rangers were staffing the Camp Muir patrol hut when they were contacted by a member of the same party who was now asking for assistance with the injured climber. The patient, Mr. Shokeir, was taken into the patrol hut, and rangers Armitage (Park Medic) and Bowman (EMT-n) performed a medical assessment. Shokeir had signs and symptoms of a probable rib fracture but was breathing adequately and appeared stable. Bowman and Armitage concluded that evacuation by litter down to Paradise would be the best course of action. At 3 p.m., Bowman took command of the incident, and Armitage and Tarantino began preparing Shokeir for evacuation by toboggan.

At approximately 5 p.m., Bowman and three guides left Camp Muir with Shokeir in a toboggan. The patient arrived at Paradise at approximately 8:05 p.m.

Analysis

Rescues are dynamic events frequently requiring diversion and redirection of resources. Patients must be triaged, and focus placed on the more critically injured. However, it is important to maintain a high level of vigilance on the less injured, as these patients can deteriorate. Rib injuries, particularly in older patients, can have a high associated morbidity and mortality, and should be treated with caution. Modern care for rib fractures is centered on early and adequate pain control to avoid complications from splinting. In alpine environments, early treatment is essential, as there is pre-existing increased demand on a person's ability to ventilate effectively. (Source: Daniel Camiccia, Wilderness Ranger.)

WYOMING

AVALANCHE – SKI MOUNTAINEERING
Grand Teton National Park, Ranger Peak

On March 7 an avalanche on 11,355-foot Ranger Peak killed ski pioneer and blogger Steve Romeo (40) and Jackson Hole Mountain Resort tram maintenance manager Chris Onufer (42) while they were ascending the mountain. The slide carried them roughly 3,000 vertical feet and buried them near the surface of debris that averaged six feet deep, the park and Bridger-Teton National Forest Avalanche Center reported. Searchers uncovered the bodies just before noon on March 8.

The two men began their trip from the Colter Bay Swim Beach parking area sometime between 5 and 7 a.m. They planned to ascend the south side of Ranger Peak from Waterfalls Canyon, then descend a steep, south-facing couloir above Wilderness Falls and continue down Waterfalls Canyon.

They started heading west across the frozen surface of Jackson Lake for approximately three miles. From the west shoreline, they continued west up and into Waterfalls Canyon for another one and a half miles to an elevation of approximately 7,400 feet. At this point in the canyon, just below Columbine Cascade, they turned north and started their steep ascent of a large avalanche path that faces south-southeast. The ascent route they chose on the south side of Ranger Peak stands out as a major drainage feature made up of steep chutes and gullies that all originate from a high point on the ridge at 10,600 feet.

At the start of the climb they were able to skin a relatively straight line up the lower-angle slope, until the gully narrowed and the slope angle reached approximately 25 to 30 degrees at an elevation of 8,600 feet. Based on the skin track found at the scene and photographs taken from the air, it is apparent that they ascended the right branch of the avalanche path. From that point on, they switchbacked up this narrow gully and kept close to the rocky cliffs bordering its east side. At an elevation of approximately 9,600 feet, their skin track traversed away from the right edge of the path and continued west across a gully into the middle of the slide path. Continuing to skin higher, the two men made three switchbacks beneath a large rock buttress. Here the slope angle averaged approximately 35 degrees, with a slight convexity in the terrain due to a rocky rib dividing the gully below. In photos taken from the air, this portion of the skin track below the rock buttress was undisturbed by the avalanche. The track stops at the southwest corner of the rock buttress near a steep chute. The last visible evidence of their skin track was found here at an elevation of 10,050 feet. At this elevation the slope increases in angle to greater than 40 degrees. It is probable that they triggered the avalanche at this point sometime between 10 a.m. and noon. The avalanche crown was about three feet deep and 300 feet across near the 10,500-foot elevation.

When Onufer failed to pick up his father, John, as scheduled at Jackson Hole Airport on the night of March 7, the father alerted authorities. GTNP rangers and Teton County Search and Rescue carried out the search and ultimate location of the party by helicopter.

Analysis

Both men were expert skiers but were undertaking an excursion into extreme terrain. Romeo authored the TetonAT.com Website, writing regularly about his alpine touring excursions and even some near misses with avalanches.

The avalanche center forecasted the danger this day as moderate, meaning human-triggered avalanches were possible. The center said soft slabs up to 14 inches deep had formed the day before.

In summary, two to three feet of new snow fell during the previous week of stormy weather. Strong west-northwest winds transported available snow and formed wind slab in east- to southeast-facing starting zones. Sunshine and warming temperatures on Sunday and Monday may have formed a sun crust on south-facing slopes at mid-elevations, and possibly at higher elevations sheltered from the cooling effects of wind. It is likely that Romeo and Onufer triggered the slab avalanche as they skinned into the starting zone where a weak layer failed above a sun crust. As the initial soft slab avalanche gained momentum, it stepped down into older layers and entrained harder snow as it traveled over rocky cliffs and through gullies. (Source: *Jackson Hole Daily*, March 9, 2012, articles by Angus M. Thuermer Jr. and by Brandon Zimmerman and Emma Breysse; Rich Baerwald, Ranger.)

(*Editor's note: These two men were longtime residents of the area and well known for their ski adventures. The newspaper articles provide an in-depth profile.*)

SLIP ON SNOW, INADEQUATE CLOTHING AND EQUIPMENT, INEXPERIENCE
Grand Teton National Park, Albright Peak

On June 6 at 4:45 p.m., I was notified by Teton Interagency Dispatch Center (TIDC) of a visitor requesting assistance near the summit of Albright Peak. The reporting party stated that her partner had slipped and fallen on snow while ascending Albright Peak, and had sustained an injury to her lower right leg. Jordan Schleicher stated that she and her partner, Danielle Mendicino (21), were ascending the east face when Mendicino slipped on snow, sliding approximately 50 to 60 feet into rocks and hitting a tree. She said they were attempting to descend the southeast face because it was snow-free, but were moving extremely slowly due to Mendicino's injury and were worried that they would not make it out before dark.

At 5 p.m., short-haul training operations were suspended at the Gros Ventre River Training Site and a briefing was conducted with the Jenny Lake ranger staff and helicopter pilot Clayton Mitchell. Mendicino and Schleicher were located from the air approximately 750 feet below the summit of Albright Peak on the south aspect. At 5:50, the helicopter landed on the summit, where ranger Scott Guenther exited the aircraft to begin descending toward Mendicino's location. Guenther arrived on scene at 6:10 p.m. and performed a patient assessment. He advised that Mendicino had suffered a disabling lower leg injury and was unable to move under her own power. He recommended an attended short-haul extrication via screamer suit. At 7:05 p.m., Guenther and Mendicino were extracted via short-haul from the scene and delivered to the landing zone at Whitegrass Meadow.

Analysis

Mendicino had slipped once earlier during the climb, but was able to catch herself quickly without incident. During her second slip, she was unable to arrest her slide on the snow surface and tumbled approximately 50 to 60 feet into rocks and hit a tree. After the accident, Mendicino and Schleicher attempted to descend by traversing onto the south face of Albright Peak in order to avoid further snow travel.

Both wore tennis shoes and had ice axes. Neither had a helmet or crampons. This was Mendicino's first season in the Tetons, and she had only been in the park for a few days. She had never used an ice axe before and did not practice self-arrest prior to the climb. Schleicher was in her third season in the Tetons and had been up Static Peak and Albright Peak (from the west side) in past years. She had not been on the east face of Albright before. She had received minimal ice axe training with a friend, but had no formal training.

The primary contributing factor in this accident was insufficient experience and equipment. Climbing a route such as this requires proper training and experience in the use of an ice axe and/or crampons. Additionally, a solid mountain boot is essential in order to properly kick steps into firm alpine snow. (Source: Ryan Schuster, Incident Commander.)

STRANDED – OFF ROUTE
Grand Teton National Park, Middle Teton

At 1:30 a.m. on July 10, SAR coordinator Marty Vidak received a call from Teton Interagency Dispatch Center (TIDC) that Eric Rohner (27) had called on his cell phone to say he had reached a point on his climb of Middle Teton where he did not feel safe going up or down. He had extra food, water, and clothing, was not injured, and was very calm. The weather forecast called for good weather that night.

Rangers Drew Hardesty and G.R. Fletcher left Lupine Meadows Rescue Cache at 5:15 a.m. They arrived at the Garnet Canyon Meadows at 7 a.m. Meanwhile, Vidak talked to Rohner at 6:40 a.m., and after questioning him further, determined that he was not in the Southwest Couloir of the Middle Teton, but probably in the vicinity of the Ellingwood Couloir. This presented a very different rescue scenario. Vidak relayed this information to the rangers in the Garnet Meadows, and Hardesty and Fletcher backtracked to the Platforms Cache to get additional climbing equipment before heading further up the canyon. They arrived at the base of the Ellingwood Couloir at about 9:20 and could not spot Rohner.

It was decided to send helicopter 20HX on a recon flight over the Middle Teton to determine Rohner's exact location before committing Hardesty and Fletcher to climbing the Ellingwood Couloir. From the helicopter, it was easy to see why Rohner was stuck. He had climbed into an area of fifth-class rock by the southeast ridge and was alone and without the means to retreat. The southeast ridge is rated Grade III 5.7 in Ortenburger and Jackson's *A Climber's Guide to the Teton Range*.

To extricate Rohner without using the helicopter would have involved sending at least four more rangers to Garnet Canyon, and a lengthy and potentially hazardous technical rescue would have been necessary. Instead, Rohner was short-hauled off the mountain using the "screamer suit," attended by a ranger.

Analysis

Eric Rohner had intended to climb the third-class Southwest Couloir of the Middle Teton. He came into the Jenny Lake Ranger Station, got a camping permit, and talked to rangers about his intended ascent route. The reasons he became so far off-route can only be guessed; he was nowhere near the Southwest Couloir route. The Middle Teton has the reputation of having an easy route to a high summit, and that reputation has lured many inexperienced climbers to technical rescues, serious accidents, and death.

When climbing on an unknown mountain, especially if the climber is relatively inexperienced, it is crucial that the climber get as much information as possible about the intended ascent. One must constantly pay attention on the ascent and descent to stay on the intended route, and also to stay in one's ability range.

Rohner made a good decision when he realized he was way out of his ability level and decided to stay put and call for help. Otherwise this rescue could have had a very dire outcome. (Source: Marty Vidak, Incident Commander.)

FALL ON ROCK, PARTY SEPARATED – CLIMBING ALONE
Grand Teton National Park, Cathedral Traverse

On July 12, Eric Tietze (31) fell about 500 feet to his death while attempting the Cathedral Traverse. He had separated from his four-person group after completing the rappels off Peak 11,840, west of Teewinot Mountain. He most likely fell while attempting the north-side traverse around the East Prong of Mt. Owen and the small tower to its east. This traverse involves fifth-class moves on complex terrain consisting of large, loose blocks.

Tietze was reported missing at 10 p.m. on July 12, and plans for the following day's search were made at that time by GTNP rescue rangers. On July 13 a complex rescue over high-risk terrain involving two GTNP contract helicopters and ground personnel ensued. Near the end of the third recon period, Tietze was spotted, wedged between snow and rock in a steep, narrow couloir that descends the northeast snowfields of Mt. Owen, below the north-side traverse. A ranger was inserted via short haul to his location, and after confirming that he was deceased, extricated him to Lupine Meadows via short haul.

Analysis

Based on the location of Tietze's body, the impact marks in the snow, and the complexity of the climbing above the couloir, ranger Chris Harder concluded that the most likely scenario that led to Tietze's demise involved a fall from the area of the chimney system. We will never know the exact cause of his fall, but the scenarios most likely involve either rockfall striking him or he may have pulled a hand or foothold off as he was negotiating the downclimb.

Eric Tietze was a capable climber, and climbing well within his means when the accident occurred. He was wearing a helmet, carried an ice axe, had proper footwear, clothing, and gear, and had climbed the route previously. He had separated from the group and was climbing unroped. During trips, he had a tendency to hike out ahead 10 or 15 minutes and then wait for the rest of the group to catch up.

Given the circumstances of this event, could anything have been done differently to prevent the unfortunate outcome? When traveling in the mountains, there is always a delicate balance between climbing roped up and unroped. Although climbing roped up may seem more secure and prevent a sudden fall, its use can drastically slow the progression of a climb and expose a party to objective dangers (rockfall, icefall, etc.) for a longer period of time. It can even turn a one-day climb into a multi-day climb. Furthermore, if a party is roped together, a fall by one climber can be disastrous to the entire party if the roped climbing is not done using some form of belay. (Source: George Montopoli, Incident Commander.)

FALL ON ROCK
Grand Teton National Park, Middle Teton

At approximately 12:05 p.m. on July 22, Justin Beldin (27) had just started his descent from the summit when he appeared to stumble or slip on loose rock and fall into a couloir. He had been in a party of three climbers who had ascended the Southwest Couloir of the Middle Teton that morning.

His two partners said they had started from the Lupine Meadows trailhead shortly before 6 a.m. They felt that their party was climbing well and all were in good spirits. They climbed through the South Fork of Garnet Canyon and up the Southwest Couloir of Middle as planned, and summited around 11:30. The partners said that Beldin made two cell phone calls from the summit, and that he was taking a lot of pictures. They both felt that he seemed to be in good physical condition on the summit. There were a number of other parties at or near the summit, and Beldin's party discussed heading down before others to avoid congestion and potential rockfall in the Southwest Couloir. They also noted the clouds and weather that appeared to be building to the west.

Beldin's partners, Parsons and Harris, started down from the summit ahead of Beldin. They did not see Beldin fall, but do think they heard something like rockfall shortly after starting down. They then said that someone from a party above shouted down to them that their partner had just fallen. They returned to the summit, but were unable to make voice or visual contact.

Analysis

At least two unassociated parties witnessed Beldin's fall. Their interviews and witness statements all confirm that Beldin appeared to fall off the peak as he began his descent. They confirm that he either stumbled while descending or slipped on loose rock that gave way beneath him. He was very near the edge of the top of the Northwest Couloir when this event happened, and he appeared to fall down face-first. Witnesses described Beldin attempting to grab onto something as he fell, but he quickly went over a steep drop out of sight. His fall was fatal.

This was a very unfortunate accident. The Southwest Couloir of the 12,804-foot Middle Teton is one of the most popular "scrambling" summit routes in the Teton Range (II, third class). This climb tends to be a reasonable objective for physically fit climbers with moderate experience in routefinding, snow travel, and rock scrambling. From the self-described skills of the members of Beldin's party, the Middle Teton via the Southwest Couloir seemed to be a reasonable objective for the party. However, this does not mean that the climb was without risk or exposure. As one reaches the summit of the Middle Teton, several couloirs converge. While portions of the summit area are relatively large and somewhat level, the final bit of climbing from the top of the Southwest Couloir traverses a narrow ridge that falls away steeply into the Northwest Couloir. (Source: Scott Guenther, Incident Commander.)

STRANDED, NOT PREPARED FOR CONDITIONS, UNDERESTIMATED DIFFICULTY
Wind River Mountains, Ellingwood Peak

On June 1 at 10:30 p.m., the Sublette County Sheriff's dispatch center received a call that two climbers, Freddie Botur (40) and his partner, were stranded three-quarters of the way up the North Arête of Ellingwood Peak. The party claimed they were not able to complete the climb due to the rotten nature of the steep snow in the final pitches. The two climbers had attempted to rappel the route, but they got their only 70-meter rope stuck, hence they were unable to ascend or descend.

Tip Top Search and Rescue (Sublette County) was paged and started making preparations for a morning rescue. A reconnaissance flight was completed at 9:20 a.m. by TTSAR members Tony Chambers and Shawn Streeter. Severe thunderstorms moved into the area, and the crew was forced to return to the Pinedale airport.

A plan was made for a short-haul rescue. The weather cleared at 3 p.m., and the SAR crew once again responded to Indian Basin, rigged for short-haul, and inserted TTSAR members Shawn Streeter and Jason Ray onto the ledge where the uninjured climbers were stranded. They were flown from the ledge at 12,500 feet in screamer suits to the established landing zone below at 10,800 feet. The operation was complete by 3:50 p.m.

Analysis

Botur and his partner underestimated the difficulty of the North Arête on Ellingwood (III 5.6). They were attempting to travel light and fast, and they were wearing plastic mountaineering boots but had no ice tools with them. The Wind Rivers in early June are often still extremely wintery. The party stated that on the more than 1,200 feet of rock they had climbed, they made very slow progress because they did not have rock shoes and the climbing was harder than they had anticipated. Also, they had not anticipated that the final three or four pitches (which are easier and less steep) would be covered with rotten snow. They reported taking a very spooky, unprotected fall on the steep snow. After making the decision to retreat, they had more difficulties with getting their rope stuck, and then running out of daylight. They had also long since run out of food and water. (Source: Tony Chambers, Tip Top Search and Rescue.)

CANADA

Editor's note: All Canadian reports in this edition were compiled from individual park reports and summaries. Robert Chisnall of the Alpine Club of Canada edited these reports and provided each analysis.

ALBERTA

SKIING – EXCEEDING ABILITIES, POOR SNOW CONDITIONS
Banff National Park, Mt. Temple, Aemmer Couloir

On February 7, at 1:50 p.m., Banff Dispatch received a call from an injured skier who had just tumbled down the Aemmer Couloir on Mt. Temple. The subject stated that he had "tomahawked" down the 600-meter couloir, after falling on his second turn. Amazingly, he was still coherent and walking slowly, but had lost one ski and was quite beat up.

Three Visitor Safety (VS) Specialists were dispatched by helicopter from Banff along with a rescue pilot from Alpine Helicopters. By 2:40 p.m., they were at Mt. Temple. Because the subject had fallen to the bottom of the couloir and landed on relatively flat ground, the rescuers were able to land nearby and load the patient directly into the helicopter. The patient was evacuated to Lake Louise, where he was transferred to EMS, and then the helicopter came back to pick up his partner and the remaining gear.

Analysis

The Aemmer Couloir is a serious ski line with 45- to 55-degree slopes at the top. When stability is good enough to go up there, the snow is often packed hard by continual sloughing, making for challenging skiing with little chance for self-arrest. In these conditions, the couloir is definitely a no-fall zone with serious consequences for a mistake.

This skier was very lucky to have "walked" away from such a big fall with only minor injuries. He was skiing at the ski hill three days later. It was a good thing he was wearing a helmet, which saved him some serious harm, and was able to use his cell phone to call for help quickly, sparing himself a cold night out or a painfully long self-evacuation.

STRANDED – EXCEEDING ABILITIES
Banff National Park, Mt. Bell

On July 10, while climbing the Northeast Ridge of Mt. Bell near the Lake Louise area, a party of two contacted Parks Canada and requested a rescue. Although they'd started early in the morning, they were only halfway up the route by 5 p.m. They stated that their slow progress was the result of one team member being very nervous and not comfortable with the terrain. Eventually, this team member did not want to move up or down the ridge, and the decision to call for a rescue was reached.

Parks Canada received the call and responded via helicopter to Mt. Bell. The climbers were located on the ridge at approximately 2,750 meters, anchored to several pinnacles. Rescue personnel landed at a staging area below, set up the rescue sling equipment under the helicopter, and were slung onto the ridge near the climbers. Rescuers then climbed approximately 25 meters to the climbers and short-roped them to a pickup location. Once this was done, the helicopter slung out two people at a time to the staging area below.

Analysis

There were no injuries involved with this incident, but simple mistakes contributed to the need for a rescue. First, overestimation of their abilities: One team member had very little experience mountaineering, and when faced with exposure on a loose, narrow ridge, the team's progress slowed to a crawl. Second, underestimation of the difficulty: The experienced team member had done the route nearly 20 years previous, and did not accurately remember how involved it was. This member stated, "I thought it was just a hike in the sky." Third, underestimation of the length of the route: They were a considerable distance from the summit at 5 p.m. when they decided to stop where they were.

The climbers did do something right, though. They stopped and accurately assessed their situation. With one person paralyzed with fear, and the second person unable to guide them up or down the route, they called for assistance. An all-night epic of trying to get off the mountain—or worse, an accident—was avoided by getting evacuated.

STRANDED – CLIMBING ALONE, FAILURE TO FOLLOW DIRECTIONS (OFF ROUTE), EXCEEDING ABILITIES
Banff National Park, Mt. Whyte

On the morning of July 20, a stranded climber called Banff Dispatch for a rescue. The climber had spent the night on a small ledge immediately below the summit of Mt. Whyte. After numerous attempts to downclimb to the Whyte-Niblock Col, the climber abandoned his descent, feeling too dehydrated and exhausted to continue.

Rescue personnel were contacted at 6:30 that morning and informed of the stranded climber. They flew from Banff and located the climber near the summit, along the north ridge. After setting up the long-line under the helicopter, one rescuer was slung in to the subject. The subject had a harness put on him, and then rescuer and subject were slung back down to the staging area below the peak.

Analysis

The climber made a smart decision to stop when he could not recognize the correct gully to descend. Although he had ascended it earlier in the day, he had not looked back to landmark key features for his return. This is a very important thing to do, as things look much different on the way down compared to when you are climbing up. Also, the subject was dehydrated and exhausted, while carrying a heavy pack. Be sure to carry appropriate amounts of food and water to get you up *and* down the mountain, as well as the equipment that will assist you to survive in the mountains. Leave behind the heavy, nonessential items if they weigh you down.

FALL ON ROCK – CAM PULLED OUT
Banff National Park, Mt. Cory

On Saturday, July 21, two climbers set off to climb a route on Bumpers Buttress west of Banff. They selected the route Short Jerky Movements, which was located above the Spasm Chasm (local name). The two climbers were quite experienced. While climbing the third pitch, the leader placed a small camming unit and had difficulty locating other sound gear placements. About five meters above this piece of protection, for an unknown reason, the leader fell. The force of the fall pulled out the small camming unit, which subsequently placed the entire force of the fall onto the belay station (factor two fall).

The climber fell a total of 35 meters and was hanging on the rope 20 meters below the belay station. The lead climber was initially unconscious, and the belayer noticed that the leader was bleeding significantly. The belayer, recognizing the severity of the situation, immediately tied off the lead climber and phoned Banff Dispatch. The dispatcher took initial information and transferred the caller to the Visitor Safety rescue leader who was on shift. The rescue leader and climber discussed the situation, and it seemed reasonable for the belayer to lower the injured climber down to the next station to wait for rescue.

After the rescue leader confirmed the location with the reporting belayer, a team of three specialists flew from Banff. Rescuers were on the scene in 40 minutes. One rescuer was long-lined into the accident location. The rescuer rigged the belay station and patient to be flown out. A second rescuer flew into the site and clipped onto the patient while the first rescuer released the patient with an Italian (Munter) hitch. The patient was flown directly to a waiting ambulance. The pilot returned for the injured climber's partner and the initial rescuer.

Analysis

The climbing team had an appropriate amount of experience to undertake such a climb. However, on occasion, experienced climbers fall off. Upon follow-up with the lead climber who fell and his belayer, it was learned that they had no recollection of why the leader fell in the first place. There are a number of possibilities: 1) rockfall, 2) breaking a hold, and 3) the climber slipped. Fortunately, the climbers had protected the anchor by redirecting the rope through the anchor. The belayer placed a quickdraw on a highpoint on the anchor to prevent the load from impacting the belayer's body directly. This maneuver likely prevented injury to the belayer. Also, the experience level of the climbers, specifically the belayer, allowed them to secure the situation to enable rescuers to efficiently extract them. This was a great example of people displaying preparedness when they have had an unlikely turn of events.

SLIP ON SNOW OR ICE – CLIMBING UNROPED, POOR CONDITIONS
Banff National Park, Mt. Lefroy

On July 27 a group of three climbers was descending the normal route on Mt. Lefroy after making a successful summit. One member of the party was making a short traverse over some icy rocks and slipped. He was not wearing crampons. He proceeded to tumble for approximately 100 meters before miraculously stopping in soft snow. He had injured his right knee and right heel. With assistance from the other two climbers, he limped his way back to the Abbot Pass hut. The accident occurred at approximately 4 p.m.

The climbing party decided to call for a rescue at approximately 9 p.m. Being so late in the day, Visitor Safety Specialists were not able to respond by helicopter until first light the following day. Since the patient had only minor injuries, it was reasonable for him to spend the night in the hut and be evacuated by helicopter at first light. Two Visitor Safety Specialists were dispatched from Banff at 5:30 a.m. and were on scene at Abbot Pass by 6:30. The Visitor Safety Specialists assisted the injured climber to the helicopter, and he was subsequently evacuated to Mineral Springs Hospital directly.

Analysis

The climbing party chose to climb Mt. Lefroy quite late in the day. However, after being interviewed, they indicated that conditions were OK for climbing, meaning the snow was not soft. More often than not, it is best to wait for the coolest period of the day to begin a climb with significant steep snow travel. However, it is unknown whether soft snow conditions were a factor in this incident. The climber made an error in judgment by making the decision to risk walking across an icy section without crampons. On the other hand, the lack of crampons may have prevented further injury to the climber during his fall. In sum, this climber was extremely lucky to have stopped in soft snow after falling 100 meters. Had the climber not stopped in that exact location, he would have likely fallen the length of the entire west face, and the outcome would not have been positive.

SLIP ON SNOW OR ICE – FAULTY USE OF CRAMPONS (CAME OFF)
Banff National Park, Mt. Lefroy

On July 31 two climbers were descending the standard route on Mt. Lefroy around 6 p.m. When they were approximately halfway down the route, one of the climber's crampons fell off. His climbing partner was 15 meters below and started to ascend back to his partner to help. As the lower climber was climbing back up, the climber with the loose crampon, who was in a bent-over position, fell over and started to slide. He knocked his partner off his feet, and they both started falling down the face. They generated a small avalanche during this ordeal, and one of the climbers describes their experience as follows: "almost stopping, then a wave of snow would wash over us and push us forward." This phenomenon occurred three or four times, and the climbers became separated during the fall. The climber higher on the slope had a minor knee injury when he came to a stop, and he began looking for his partner, whom he located further down the slope. His partner was unconscious and had sustained a severe head injury. It also appeared that his helmet had come off during the fall.

The incident was witnessed by people staying in the Abbot Pass Hut. A small team of climbers went to assist the fallen climbing party. They brought with them a stretcher (stationed at the hut) and some first-aid supplies. They were able to place the patient in the stretcher and carry him down-slope approximately 150 meters to a flat area, where they waited for rescue. The incident was called in by somebody who remained at the hut. This person had to climb up behind the outhouse to obtain a cell phone signal, as there is very poor reception at the hut itself.

After calling Banff Dispatch, the caller was transferred to the rescue leader (RL) on shift. The rescue leader collected information and mustered a crew of Visitor Safety Specialists from Banff and Lake Louise.

A team of four specialists was airborne approximately 45 minutes after the accident occurred. One specialist maintained staging logistics and security at the Chateau Lake Louise parking area while two other specialists responded to Abbot Pass with the rescue leader. The injured climber was located quickly. However, a thunderstorm was brewing just behind the pass. After an initial assessment, a plan was made to act quickly, safely, and professionally in order to minimize the chance of the patient being caught out overnight in a storm. One specialist was dropped at the patient's location with gear to prepare for loading directly into the helicopter. The second specialist was flown down to the hut to locate the second injured climber, whose location and condition were unknown at that time.

While this was occurring, the RL flew down to the Plain of Six Glaciers Tea House to configure the helicopter to receive a horizontal patient with the pilot. In the time it took the rescue pilot and RL to configure the helicopter, the specialist on scene with the patient was ready for pickup. The RL came back with the pilot to the scene, and the patient was loaded efficiently. The RL and the specialist traded places. The RL remained on scene with the other climbers, and the specialist flew down to the staging area with the patient (where the patient was transferred to Banff EMS). The RL took the group down to the hut to meet up with the other injured climber and specialist. The rest of the Parks Canada staff and the injured climber remained at the hut until the storm passed, at which point they were all flown down to Lake Louise.

Analysis

It is unknown what caused the climber to fall specifically. However, crampons falling off mid-route is something to be avoided. Always ensure that safety equipment such as crampons is secured tightly. Checking twice and having the situational awareness to anticipate this type of incident likely would have prevented such an accident.

This accident was initially responded to by a group of climbers nearby. Parks Canada cautions climbers about taking it upon themselves to rescue and assist other parties who find themselves in trouble. We do recognize that in some cases, actions of nearby climbers can make a big difference in the outcome for people who have had accidents. Nevertheless, if those actions are not thought through critically, vigilant rescuers can become victims, making the problem twice as big as it originally was. Therefore, Parks Canada urges climbers to think critically about situations and come up with a strong rationale for responding to accidents in their immediate vicinity. Rest assured that if the decision is made not to respond based on reasons of personal safety, climbers will not be held responsible for not responding. Parks Canada has professional rescue staff that will ultimately deal with all mountain-related accidents. Using common sense and critical thinking, climbers need to make their own decision whether to respond to climbing accidents in their immediate vicinity.

To be clear, in the case of this rescue, the actions taken by the climbers at the hut were reasonable and safe, and likely contributed to a better outcome for the climber who had fallen. Good job!

(*Editor's note: Recent articles, online discussions, rescue data, and current trends indicate there is a need for climbers to be self-reliant and well versed in improvised partner and self-rescue. Barring injuries and overwhelming circumstances, a number of problematic situations can be handled independently by experienced and practiced climbing teams.*)

STRANDED – EXCEEDING ABILITIES, FAILURE TO FOLLOW DIRECTIONS (OFF ROUTE), DARKNESS, INADEQUATE EQUIPMENT/CLOTHING
Banff National Park, Tunnel Mountain

On August 2 two climbers who were relatively inexperienced started late in the day on a route that they thought was Ballista. Ballista is a bolted sport climb on the southeast face of Tunnel Mountain. They were climbing very slowly, and at one point one of the climbers took a 10-meter lead fall but sustained no injuries. They continued to climb, but eventually it became too dark to continue. They called Banff Dispatch and were transferred to the rescue leader on shift. They tried to describe their position to the rescue leader, but some of the details did not immediately add up. However, they were certain they were only one pitch from the top.

Two Visitor Safety Specialists responded by hiking up the backside of Tunnel Mountain. It took some time to locate the stranded climbers, but a combination of flashing cell phone screens and yelling brought the specialists in line with the climbers. At this point, the specialists, who are intimately familiar with climbing routes in Banff National Park, discovered they were in fact on a route called Tatonka, which is closer to Gooseberry. After making a plan, one specialist was lowered down to the two climbers. The specialist on top hauled the climbers separately up to the top, and subsequently the specialist who was lowered down jumared back up. The specialists then accompanied the two climbers to the trailhead.

Analysis

The climbers were unprepared and chose an objective that was beyond their ability. Additionally, the climbers did not have helmets or headlamps for their ascent, both of which are crucial equipment, especially the headlamps if you are starting late in the day. Their inexperience was demonstrated by the fact that they did not do enough research on their objective. Climbers are advised to take a proper instructional course from a member of the Association of Canadian Mountain Guides (the only group that is permitted to teach climbing in the national parks). The acquisition of climbing and mountaineering competency involves a slow apprenticeship. It takes time and patience to be able to climb harder and more obscure objectives. Therefore, raising the grade, length, and commitment factor in small increments is prudent.

RAPPEL ERROR/FAILURE, CLIMBING ALONE, EXCEEDING ABILITIES, FAILURE TO FOLLOW DIRECTIONS (OFF ROUTE), INADEQUATE PROTECTION
Banff National Park, Castle Mountain

A climber left Calgary on the morning of August 4, telling his wife that he was going to Castle Mountain. He did not return home that evening. Banff Dispatch was contacted the following morning by a friend of the missing climber. The friend reported that the subject was likely going to climb Eisenhower Tower on Castle Mountain, and that he was supposed to have met them on the morning of August 5 to climb something else.

The report was transferred to a Visitor Safety (VS) Specialist, and a trailhead search for the subject's vehicle was performed. His vehicle was located at the Castle Lookout Trailhead. This is the standard parking area for some routes on Castle, but not for Eisenhower Tower. An aerial, ground, and dog search commenced, and VS crews searched the high-probability areas throughout the day. The search was called off at dark with no clues regarding the missing person.

On August 6 the aerial, ground, and dog search continued. More searchers were called in, and an expanded search strategy was developed. Research was conducted on the subject's profile and where he might be expected to go. The subject was a somewhat experienced scrambler but had just started climbing recently, and he had never done a multi-pitch climb. However, his friends described him as a skilled and fearless scrambler who liked to "go straight up to the peak." He did not usually do any research on his objectives, but was usually bold enough to reach the summit, even if off route. His friends said that he knew about Eisenhower Tower and really wanted to climb it. However, he had parked in the wrong spot for Eisenhower. He had also left fairly late, and would have been climbing on Castle in the heat of a hot summer day. This information helped VS Specialists form a picture of where the subject may have gone. Still, the subject was not found.

On the afternoon of August 7 the subject was finally located by helicopter on the upper reaches of Castle Mountain (near Bass Buttress). He was in a tight gully feature where he was difficult to see from the air. He was in the vicinity of an established route, but not on it. The subject appeared to have rappelled off the ends of his rope and had fallen about 40 meters. The subject appeared to be deceased. A recovery attempt was made in the afternoon but was aborted due to high winds.

On August 8 three VS Specialists recovered the body in the early morning via a sling rescue. This was a complex operation involving rope work in technical terrain and precision flying. The VS specialists were slung onto a nearby ledge, from where they climbed easy terrain until they were above the deceased. One of the VS specialists was lowered to the deceased to attach a rope and prepare the body for transport. The helicopter arrived at the original ledge system, the rope was attached to the rescue line, and the body was slung off using approximately 100 meters of line. This approach was taken because the gully was too tight for the helicopter to fly directly above the accident site. The winds were calm in the early morning, which made the operation much safer for everyone involved.

Analysis

This was an extended search and recovery operation for the VS Specialists. All of the highest probability areas were in technical terrain, which made it difficult to use larger groups of untrained searchers. Although much of the terrain could be seen from the air, numerous tight gullies along the cliff face made effective airborne searching difficult. The subject profile also left it very open as to where he may have gone. Unfortunately, this search did not end with a positive outcome.

VS Specialists pieced together the subject's approximate itinerary from pictures found on his camera. Amazingly, the subject had summited Castle by climbing somewhere in the vicinity of Bass Buttress. He may have been on the route, but this is unlikely. Most likely he climbed one of the gully features to the summit of Castle. This is an impressive feat, as it would involve fifth-class climbing in loose, untraveled terrain without the protection of a rope. The subject decided to rappel the face he had climbed, and had made three or four rappels before he got into trouble. He had no gear to build anchors; he was following off-route anchor stations. He had no knots in the ends of his rope when he found himself dangling above a steep, sheer wall with little opportunity for natural anchors. He was most likely searching for the next anchor when he rappelled off the ends of his ropes. He fell approximately 40 meters into the gully and most likely died on impact.

There are a few lessons we can learn from this:

1. Tell someone where you are going and when you expect to return. This is a big one, and although it may not have changed the outcome in this case, the

subject would have been found in much less time. This is especially important when climbing alone.

2. Carry a communication device.

3. Research your objective. Find out where established routes and descents are, what gear to bring, and how long it should take. There are multiple established descents off Castle, including a walk-off and an easy scramble with a few 30-meter rappels off bolted stations. Sadly, these are located within 300 meters of where the subject perished.

4. Get proper training and instruction before heading out on your own.

It was quite a feat to pioneer a new route and descent on Castle solo. It is unfortunate that it ended with a rappelling accident that could have been avoided by simply tying knots in the ends of the ropes.

(Editor's note: Using an autoblock backup system can prevent rappel mishaps of this kind. In addition, anyone rappelling multi-pitch routes should have the basic knowledge and skill to improvise with the limited gear they carry and ascend their rappel lines, in case their rope is too short or they cannot find the next rappel station.)

FALLING ROCK
Banff National Park, Division Peak

As a part of a climbing camp set up in Icefall Brook, a party of six was traversing Division Peak near the Lyell Icefields on August 5. While descending the final peak, a member of the party was hit by rockfall on the arm and sustained a compound fracture. One member of the party continued back to camp to call for rescue by satellite phone, while the four others stayed with the injured climber and activated their SPOT device.

Parks Canada was notified of the incident at approximately 3 p.m. The Visitor Safety team was already engaged in two other search and rescue operations, so a member of Kananaskis Public Safety was requested to join the Parks Canada rescue leader. The Kananaskis Public Safety member rendezvoused with Parks Canada at Castle Junction by helicopter, and the team then continued to Lake Louise to pick up gear. From Lake Louise they were en route to the Lyell Icefields.

The climbing team was quickly located, and the rescue leader formulated a plan. The Parks Canada rescuer slung into the site and relayed back to the other rescuer the equipment needed to accomplish the rescue. The other team member then slung into the site. The patient was packaged quickly and was slung out to the staging area with the Kananaskis Public Safety member. The four other climbers were subsequently sent out via sling to the staging area, followed by the rescue leader, who came last. The uninjured climbers were flown back to their camp because it was very late in the day. The injured climber was flown back to Lake Louise to meet Banff EMS with the rescue team.

Analysis

Rockfall is common in the Canadian Rockies. Therefore, careful positioning of climbers and routefinding is required. The experience level of the group is unknown. However, it appeared that they dealt with the situation appropriately. They administered first aid and placed a call for help via two different methods to ensure that a rescue was launched.

LEAD FALL ON ROCK
Banff National Park, Mt. Temple, East Ridge

On August 11 two climbers were making an attempt on the East Ridge of Mt. Temple. As the lead climber was nearing the top of the Big Step, he fell approximately three to five meters and broke his right ankle. His partner took over the lead, and the two climbers made it to a relatively flat area on top of the Big Step and called for rescue.

Two Visitor Safety Specialists were dispatched from Banff. They flew over the accident location so the pilot could do a power check with the helicopter and determine the wind level. The specialists then staged out of the field next to Moraine Lake Lodge. The rescue leader was slung to the site to prepare the injured subject. The second rescuer then slung up to the accident site and hooked onto the injured climber, who had been prepared by the rescue leader. The second rescuer and the injured climber were flown down to staging. The helicopter made a return trip for the uninjured climber and the rescue leader. Once all people were at the staging area, the uninjured climber was driven back to his vehicle by a park warden, and the injured climber was loaded into the helicopter and flown directly to Mineral Springs Hospital in Banff.

Analysis

Occasionally, well-prepared climbers fall off. These two climbers were experienced, and the East Ridge of Temple was an appropriate undertaking for them. They chose a day with good weather and conditions, which also showed that they displayed good judgment. The Rockies are inherently loose, and occasionally things happen and people can fall. Despite their bad luck, they were well prepared, which facilitated a smooth rescue.

SLIP ON SNOW OR ICE, STRANDED – EXCEEDING ABILITIES
Banff National Park, Mt. Victoria, East Face

On September 9 two experienced climbers decided to turn around before making the summit of Mt. Victoria. On their descent, the female member of the climbing team fell and slid down the northeast face for approximately 45 meters. She miraculously managed to self-arrest. Her climbing partner was unable to assist her. He went down to the hut and called Banff Dispatch.

A team of two Visitor Safety Specialists was dispatched from Banff. They made several unsuccessful attempts to access the stranded climber's location. Due to poor visibility and strong winds, they were forced to land at the Plain of Six Glaciers Tea House. Eventually, they returned to Lake Louise to refuel, and then they made a successful trip to get the team members into Abbot Pass. The two rescuers were able to climb up and meet the non-stranded male member of the climbing team. They left him at that location and continued up, searching for the stranded climber. They made voice contact at nightfall. The rescuers placed a piton anchor in the rock above the patient, who was found 45 meters below ridgeline on the northeast face. One rescuer was lowered down and clipped into the stranded climber's harness. The rescuer and stranded climber were then belayed back up to the ridgeline. From here, the rescue team guided the uninjured climber back down to her climbing partner, now in complete darkness. Each rescuer guided one member of the climbing team down to the Abbot Pass Hut, where they all spent the night. The next day, a helicopter picked up the climbers, along with the rescuers, and flew them back to Lake Louise.

Analysis

The climbing party admitted that they were unprepared and under-experienced for climbing Mt. Victoria. Equally important, when things went wrong, they lacked the skills to be able to rectify their situation. Furthermore, they explained that they had learned about climbing from reading books. The lack of formal instruction and/or genuine mentorship from an experienced person was the major contributing factor that led them into their predicament on Victoria.

LEAD FALL ON ROCK – PROTECTION PULLED OUT
Ha Ling Peak (Chinaman's Peak), Northeast Ridge

On July 8 a party of two was ascending the Northeast Ridge (5.6) of Ha Ling Peak. The leader climbed off route and subsequently fell 10 meters, pulling a cam in the process. Kananaskis Public Safety rescuers slung the climbers from the face and transferred care to EMS. The injured leader sustained abrasions, lacerations, and a fracture.

Analysis

It was deemed that the leader failed to follow route directions. Risks can be reduced with better route knowledge and by being able to recognize when the climbing difficulties exceed the grade. If feasible, the leader should place adequate gear. This may not have been possible in this case. Getting off route is a frequent occurrence in the Rockies. Being able to recognize and follow an established route is a skill leaders acquire through experience.

LEAD FALL ON ROCK – FAILURE TO FOLLOW DIRECTIONS (OFF ROUTE), POOR POSITION
Yamnuska, Bottleneck

On July 2, a party of two was off route near the fifth pitch of Bottleneck on Yamnuska. A foot slipped and the leader fell 15 to 20 meters. All of the lead gear held and stopped the fall. However, one of the party's double ropes sustained damage. The leader was secured, and the belayer rappelled to the fallen climber to give first aid and to call for a rescue. Both members of the team were slung off the face by the Kananaskis Public Safety rescue team. The patient was transported to hospital by air ambulance. The injured party sustained a fracture.

Analysis

In retrospect, it can be seen that the party was slightly off route and the leader climbed into a poor position. It was fortunate that the lead gear held. Exposure to this kind of mishap can be reduced through better routefinding skills and by recognizing the consequences of loose terrain.

FALLING ROCK – FAILURE TO FOLLOW DIRECTIONS (OFF ROUTE), FAILURE TO TEST HOLDS
Yamnuska, Directissima

This incident occurred on September 18. While climbing the Directissima Route on Yamnuska, the leader pulled off a large block, hitting the belayer. The belayer was knocked unconscious for 20 to 25 seconds before becoming responsive. He was bleeding with a head injury. Rescue personnel arrived from both Kananaskis Public Safety and Banff National Park to evacuate the patient. The injured party was slung off and transferred to hospital via air ambulance. The injured belayer sustained a laceration and a concussion.

Analysis

The leader was off route, failed to follow directions, and did not test the rock for loose holds. Proactive anticipation of risks requires leaders to recognize poor rock quality and to know when they are off route.

INJURED SCRAMBLER
Waterton Lakes National Park, Mt. Crandell

Around 8:30 a.m. on July 12, one scrambler in a group of five dislocated his shoulder while climbing on Tick Ridge on Mt. Crandell. The climber did not fall and was able to reverse his moves onto lower-angle terrain, but was in a great deal of pain. After some discussion, a smart phone was used to find a number for the Waterton Lakes National Park wardens using a Google search. With no answer at a now-unused number found on the Internet, 911 was called and a connection made to the Lethbridge Dispatch Centre and the Visitor Safety team in Waterton Lakes National Park.

Visitor Safety received the call at 9:10 a.m. The GPS coordinates from the party helped confirm their location. The party had used a triangular sling to support the injury and minimize further aggravation. Visitor Safety advised the party that if the injury and terrain allowed, they should move down the mountain slightly to become more visible and easier to access. The party was given the cell phone number of the rescue leader and asked to call if they had any problems or further questions.

By 10:20 a.m., Bighorn Helicopters arrived from Cranbrook and a reconnaissance flight was conducted. Because of the open spot chosen by the party and their use of high-visibility flagging tape, it was easy for the Visitor Safety technicians to find the party and determine a plan of action. A phone call was then made to the group to check on the patient's condition, inform them of the plan of action, and advise them to stay off to the side of the clearing to avoid any rockfall generated by the helicopter.

At 10:35 the first rescuer landed on the site and assessed the patient. A second rescuer was flown in immediately with a Bauman Bag and vacuum mattress. The patient was able to walk to a flat spot and position himself on the vacuum mattress for packaging. Even with gentle handling the patient was in extreme pain, and the slightest contact or movement caused distress. The patient was secured laterally to the vacuum mattress and flown to the helipad at 11 a.m., where he was transferred to waiting Waterton EMS staff and brought to the Cardston Hospital for treatment.

Excess equipment was slung off of the ridge, and the second Visitor Safety technician descended with the remaining four members of the party, reaching the road by 12:25 p.m.

Analysis

Even the strongest and most experienced mountaineers can be injured unexpectedly. If an injury causes a fall when moving unroped, the consequences can be exceptionally severe. Carrying basic first-aid supplies allowed this party to stabilize the injured limb, which undoubtedly contributed to the patient's comfort. The use of a cell phone to call for advice in this situation was a critical move. It is always a good idea to call for help or advice. Although it was only an upper-body injury and the patient could walk a short distance in simple terrain, it would have been hazardous to both the patient and the rest of his party to descend the rough terrain to the road. Some of the most serious incidents in the mountains occur as a result of problems compounding to a point where things are out of control, when early correction may have avoided further mishap. Remaining available for further telephone contact allowed rescuers to stay up to the minute on the patient's condition and inform the scramblers about relevant hazards seen at the rescue site from the air. The use of high-visibility flagging tape assisted the rescue team and pilot to see the party and gave the pilot some information on local winds at the rescue site.

If this party had researched the current emergency phone number prior to leaving, their rescue would have happened even sooner. A phone number that was in use five years ago in the back of the guidebook or written on some random Internet site may no longer work. If in doubt, call before you go to check the number, and make sure that all members of your party know how to call for help in an emergency. The Waterton Park emergency number is currently 403-859-2636.

BRITISH COLUMBIA

SLIP ON SNOW – CLIMBING UNROPED, INADEQUATE OR NO PROTECTION, FAILURE TO TEST HOLDS, NO HELMET, POOR POSITION, UNABLE TO SELF-ARREST
Vancouver Island, Strathcona Park, Rambler Peak, El Piveto Mountain, and Wolf-Cervus Divide

The accident occurred on August 2 during a descent from the shoulder of Rambler Peak, heading toward El Piveto Mountain. This was day two of a planned six-day mountaineering traverse of the Wolf-Cervus Divide, and all members had full packs. DC and CE had just completed an ascent of Rambler Peak via the Spiral Staircase route, and they met with JY at the Rambler shoulder. It was approximately 2:30 p.m., and the descent involved weaving down snow slopes of 30 to 40 degrees between bluff-like rock sections. All members were using ice axes, but not wearing helmets or crampons. JY was familiar with the route, having previously done part of the traverse, and was out in lead. At one point CE had a loss of footing, and was able to self-arrest. However, it was apparent that the snow was quite soft, and arresting was difficult. About five minutes after this slip, JY was transitioning into a steeper stretch of snow (35 to 40 degrees) when he slipped. He slid for 30 to 40 feet on snow, during which time he made several unsuccessful attempts to self-arrest. He then hit a steep rock bluff and fell for another 30 to 40 feet of near free fall.

JY was unresponsive to calls and was not visible, as he had plunged over the cliff. DC directed CE to move to safer terrain where she could wait, and then DC proceeded down the slope to where JY had fallen. It took maybe five minutes to descend to JY, and he was found at the base of the slope, face-down in a moat, conscious. JY had suffered numerous abrasions and lacerations, including large gashes on his head and knee, and he was significantly disoriented. (He did not know where he was or what he was doing.) DC was able to remove JY's pack and move him into a stable location in the moat. DC performed an assessment of JY's condition, and was able to determine that JY had broken several ribs and, while conscious, was unable to move. At that point DC deployed a distress call using a SPOT device.

While waiting for a response to the distress call, DC attended to JY's surface wounds, monitored his condition, and kept him warm with dry clothes and a sleeping bag. Approximately 45 minutes after the distress signal had been sent, an RCMP helicopter arrived and assessed the situation. There were no suitable landing spots near the accident, but DC was able to communicate the nature of the issue (broken ribs) to the RCMP. They advised that they were seeking additional support for a rescue. To facilitate a rescue, DC returned to CE and set up a rappel station to enable the team to regroup with JY.

Approximately one hour later, a Cormorant helicopter with CFB Comox arrived and deployed two SAR techs via winch and long-line. They provided additional first aid to JY, and coordinated the air evacuation of all three team members. From CFB Comox, JY was transported to the hospital in Comox, where he was diagnosed with a punctured lung, six broken ribs, and several surface wounds.

Analysis

The online accident report cites the following contributory factors: climbing unroped, inadequate or no protection, failure to test holds, no helmet, poor position, and soft snow making self-arrest not feasible. Concern over snow conditions should have been communicated, and increased diligence around footing and self-belays may have checked the initial slip. Route options were limited, but perhaps an alternate route might have had less exposure to poor run-outs.

(*Editor's note: Attempting to self-arrest while wearing crampons can cause injury. On the other hand, could crampons have initially prevented the fall?*)

LEAD FALL ON ROCK, FALLING ROCK – INADEQUATE PROTECTION, FAILURE TO TEST HOLDS
Mt. Robson Provincial Park, Mt. Geikie

On August 15 four experienced climbers were climbing the south face of Mt. Geikie. This is a remote, alpine-style rock climb located at the western portion of the Rampart Mountains in Tonquin Valley. They were climbing roped in teams of two, both parties staying in close proximity to each other. At approximately 10 a.m., one of the climbers was leading a 5.4 pitch when the half-car-sized block he was standing on released, causing him to fall along with it. Tumbling with the large rock, he fell 20 meters before his belayer caught him just as he hit a ledge with the large rock. The rock exploded, spreading shrapnel. The belayer was hit by rockfall, injuring him and forcing him off the ledge. The belayer suffered three broken ribs.

This impact ledge was adjacent to the second party. A third climber, who was standing near the ledge where the block impacted and where the lead climber came to rest, suffered lacerations to his head. He also sustained soft-tissue damage to his ankle where a falling rock penetrated his boot. The fourth climber escaped unscathed. The lead climber suffered massive internal injuries, never regained consciousness, and eventually stopped breathing. They attempted to call out with a satellite phone but had no reception. Both climbing parties' ropes were damaged. They salvaged what they could and performed short rappels to descend. Using the satellite phone, emergency contact was attempted several times during the descent with no reception.

They returned to base camp at 8:50 p.m. and established satellite reception. They called Jasper National Parks Emergency Dispatch to report the incident. At dusk a helicopter was launched from Yellowhead Helicopters in Valemount to fly directly to their camp. The helicopter had just enough daylight to retrieve one person and return to Valemount in the dark. A Jasper National Parks rescue team helicoptered to the camp at first light. The remaining two people were evacuated, and the lead climber was heli-slung off the face and pronounced deceased.

Analysis

This was an unfortunate rockfall accident involving an experienced party. The victim was a longtime Alpine Club of Canada member who had climbed all of the 11,000-foot peaks in the Canadian Rockies. He likely fell as far as he did for a couple of reasons. The belayer was unable to catch the fall because he was hit by rocks, injured, and knocked off his ledge. Also, the victim likely had not put in much protection, as he was on easier 5.4 climbing terrain.

STATISTICAL TABLES

TABLE I
REPORTED MOUNTAINEERING ACCIDENTS

Year	Number of Accidents Reported		Total Persons Involved		Injured		Fatalities	
	USA	CAN	USA	CAN	USA	CAN	USA	CAN
1951	15	n/a	22	n/a	11	n/a	3	n/a
1952	31	n/a	35	n/a	17	n/a	13	n/a
1953	24	n/a	27	n/a	12	n/a	12	n/a
1954	31	n/a	41	n/a	31	n/a	8	n/a
1955	34	n/a	39	n/a	28	n/a	6	n/a
1956	46	n/a	72	n/a	54	n/a	13	n/a
1957	45	n/a	53	n/a	28	n/a	18	n/a
1958	32	n/a	39	n/a	23	n/a	11	n/a
1959	42	2	56	2	31	0	19	2
1960	47	4	64	12	37	8	19	4
1961	49	9	61	14	45	10	14	4
1962	71	1	90	1	64	0	19	1
1963	68	11	79	12	47	10	19	2
1964	53	11	65	16	44	10	14	3
1965	72	0	90	0	59	0	21	0
1966	67	7	80	9	52	6	16	3
1967	74	10	110	14	63	7	33	5
1968	70	13	87	19	43	12	27	5
1969	94	11	125	17	66	9	29	2
1970	129	11	174	11	88	5	15	5
1971	110	17	138	29	76	11	31	7
1972	141	29	184	42	98	17	49	13
1973	108	6	131	6	85	4	36	2
1974	96	7	177	50	75	1	26	5
1975	78	7	158	22	66	8	19	2
1976	137	16	303	31	210	9	53	6
1977	121	30	277	49	106	21	32	11
1978	118	17	221	19	85	6	42	10
1979	100	36	137	54	83	17	40	19
1980	191	29	295	85	124	26	33	8

Year	Number of Accidents Reported		Total Persons Involved		Injured		Fatalities	
	USA	CAN	USA	CAN	USA	CAN	USA	CAN
1981	97	43	223	119	80	39	39	6
1982	140	48	305	126	120	43	24	14
1983	187	29	442	76	169	26	37	7
1984	182	26	459	63	174	15	26	6
1985	195	27	403	62	190	22	17	3
1986	203	31	406	80	182	25	37	14
1987	192	25	377	79	140	23	32	9
1988	156	18	288	44	155	18	24	4
1989	141	18	272	36	124	11	17	9
1990	136	25	245	50	125	24	24	4
1991	169	20	302	66	147	11	18	6
1992	175	17	351	45	144	11	43	6
1993	132	27	274	50	121	17	21	1
1994	158	25	335	58	131	25	27	5
1995	168	24	353	50	134	18	37	7
1996	139	28	261	59	100	16	31	6
1997	158	35	323	87	148	24	31	13
1998	138	24	281	55	138	18	20	1
1999	123	29	248	69	91	20	17	10
2000	150	23	301	36	121	23	24	7
2001	150	22	276	47	138	14	16	2
2002	139	27	295	29	105	23	34	6
2003	118	29	231	32	105	22	18	6
2004	160	35	311	30	140	16	35	14
2005	111	19	176	41	85	14	34	7
2006	109	n/a	227	n/a	89	n/a	21	n/a
2007	113	n/a	211	n/a	95	n/a	15	n/a
2008	112	n/a	203	n/a	96	n/a	19	n/a
2009	126	n/a	240	n/a	112	n/a	23	n/a
2010	185	n/a	389	n/a	151	n/a	34	n/a
2011*	157	n/a	348	n/a	109	n/a	29	n/a
2012	140	15	309	36	121	12	30	2
Totals:	7,053	973	13,091	2,039	5,931	727	1,544	294

*A rappel error fatality that happened in Utah in 2011 was added. See page 81.

TABLE II
ACCIDENTS BY LOCATION

Geographical Districts	1951–2011 Number of Accidents	Deaths	Total Persons Involved	2012 Number of Accidents	Deaths	Total Persons Involved
Canada*						
Alberta	520	142	1033	13	1	29
British Columbia	317	119	641	2	1	7
Yukon Territory	37	28	77	n/a	n/a	n/a
New Brunswick	1	0	0	n/a	n/a	n/a
Ontario	37	9	67	n/a	n/a	n/a
Quebec	31	10	63	n/a	n/a	n/a
East Arctic	8	2	21	n/a	n/a	n/a
West Arctic	2	2	2	n/a	n/a	n/a
Practice Cliffs[1]	20	2	36	n/a	n/a	n/a
United States						
Alaska	570	210	986	14	6	44
Arizona, Nevada, Texas	106	18	196	5	2	11
Atlantic–North	1060	151	1824	18	1	45
Atlantic–South	169	35	307	16	5	41
California	1406	305	762	35	2	60
Central	137	18	225	0	0	0
Colorado	872	229	2524	18	41	15
Montana, Idaho, South Dakota	90	35	148	1	1	2
Oregon	224	119	509	9	2	14
Utah, New Mex.	188	62	345	4	2	7
Washington	1092	334	1025	10	1	29
Wyoming	601	144	1116	7	4	13

*No data from 2006-2011, includes new data from 2012

[1]This category includes bouldering, artificial climbing walls, buildings, and so forth. These are also added to the count of each province, but not to the total count, though that error has been made in previous years. The Practice Cliffs category has been removed from the U.S. data.

TABLE III
ACCIDENTS BY CAUSE

	1951–2011 USA	1959–2005 CAN.	2012 USA	2012 CAN.
Terrain				
Rock	4839	528	100	11
Snow	2510	355	38	3
Ice	286	15	2	0
River	15	3	0	0
Unknown	22	10	0	0
Ascent or Descent				
Ascent	3894	587	86	8
Descent	1173	371	50	6
Unknown	257	13	2	0
Other[1]	14	0	2	0
Immediate Cause				
Fall or slip on rock	3829	290	72	5
Slip on snow or ice	1094	207	23	3
Falling rock, ice, or object	659	137	8	3
Exceeding abilities	564	32	13	4
Illness[2]	437	26	5	0
Stranded	376	53	10	4
Avalanche	312	127	5	0
Rappel Failure/Error[3]	328	47	17	1
Exposure	279	14	1	0
Loss of control/glissade	224	17	1	0
Nut/chock pulled out	261	9	9	2
Failure to follow route	226	30	13	5
Fall into crevasse/moat	174	50	2	0
Faulty use of crampons	118	6	2	1
Piton/ice screw pulled out	95	13	0	0
Ascending too fast	73	0	0	0
Skiing[4]	66	11	1	0
Lightning	47	7	0	0
Equipment failure	16	3	0	0

	1951–2011 USA	1959–2005 CAN.	2012 USA	2012 CAN.
Other[5]	573	37	14	1
Unknown	61	10	0	0
Contributory Causes				
Climbing unroped	1041	165	11	2
Exceeding abilities	975	202	17	1
Placed no/inadequate protection	830	96	24	3
Inadequate equipment/ clothing	724	70	8	1
Weather	511	67	10	0
Climbing alone	426	69	9	1
No hard hat	363	71	7	1
Inadequate belay[3]	253	28	9	0
Nut/chock pulled out	215	32	2	0
Poor position	215	20	8	1
Darkness	168	21	0	0
Party separated	124	12	4	0
Failure to test holds	108	32	0	5
Piton/ice screw pulled out	86	13	0	0
Failed to follow directions	70	12	0	0
Exposure	66	16	0	0
Illness[2]	40	9	0	0
Equipment failure	13	7	0	0
Other[5]	299	100	2	0
Age of Individuals				
Under 15	1247	12	1	0
15-20	1314	203	7	1
21-25	1480	257	30	0
26-30	1401	211	27	0
31-35	2082	114	21	1
36-50	1420	143	32	0
Over 50	337	31	25	1
Unknown	2097	530	33	19
Experience Level				
None/Little	1872	304	25	3
Moderate (1 to 3 years)	1704	354	29	2

	1951–2011 USA	1959–2005 CAN.	2012 USA	2012 CAN.
Experienced	2243	440	53	6
Unknown	2305	559	69	11
Month of Year				
January	250	25	6	0
February	224	55	6	0
March	346	68	10	0
April	442	39	14	0
May	977	62	17	0
June	1182	70	24	0
July	1223	254	28	7
August	1130	184	4	6
September	2011	75	16	1
October	489	42	9	0
November	223	20	3	0
December	120	24	3	0
Unknown	20	1	0	0
Type of Injury/Illness *Data since 1984				
Fracture	1475	223	46	6
Laceration	787	71	18	4
Abrasion	389	76	7	1
Bruise	550	83	18	1
Sprain/strain	423	33	27	2
Concussion	286	28	17	2
Hypothermia	171	16	5	0
Frostbite	140	12	7	0
Dislocation	152	16	5	0
Puncture	53	13	0	0
Acute Mountain Sickness	48	0	0	0
HAPE	83	0	2	0
HACE	30	0	1	0
Other[6]	380	49	11	1
None	306	188	19	7

N.B. Data change: The 1986 and 1997 editions had some repeat data from previous years. The corrections are reflected in the cumulative data.

[1] Some accidents happen when climbers are at the top or bottom of a route, not climbing. They may be setting up a belay or rappel, or are just not anchored when they fall. This category was created in 2001. The category "unknown" is primarily because of solo climbers.

[2] These illnesses/injuries, which led directly or indirectly to the accident, included: atypical HACE; HAPE (2); cardiac conditions (3); fatigue/exhaustion (2); dehydration (3); did not reveal medical conditions to guides.

[3] These included: inadequate anchor (3); rope slid through device (2); rope too short; rappelled off end–no knot (3); simul-rappel; unfinished tie-in knot; inadequate backup; too much slack in belay rope; tangled rappel rope in harness.

[4] This category was set up originally for ski mountaineering. Some extreme-ski incidents qualify. Back-country ski touring or snowshoeing incidents—even if avalanched—are not in the data.

[5] These included: poor or miscommunication (3); failure to self-arrest (4); cam dislodged boulder; pulled rock onto himself; dislodged hand or foothold (3); inadequate food/water (3); lost one crampon; rope not secured to harness; distraction; did not heed avalanche warning.

[6] These included: dehydration; blunt force trauma (4); fatigue/exhaustion; internal injuries; cardiac (3); unspecified back injury (3); leg amputated; hemopneumothorax; pneumothorax (2) dehydration (3); collapsed lung; lacerated (1) and ruptured (1) spleen; rope burn.

Editor's note: Under the category "other," many of the particular items will have been recorded under a general category. For example, the climber who dislodges a rock that falls on another climber would be coded as "Falling Rock/Object." A climber who has a hand or foothold come loose and falls would be coded as "Fall On Rock" and "Other"–and most often includes "Failure To Test Holds." Rappel and belay errors are also recorded as "Fall on Rock," and so forth.

The graphs below were originally created by Benjamin Pontecorvo and were modified with data through 2012.

ACCIDENTS BY TERRAIN

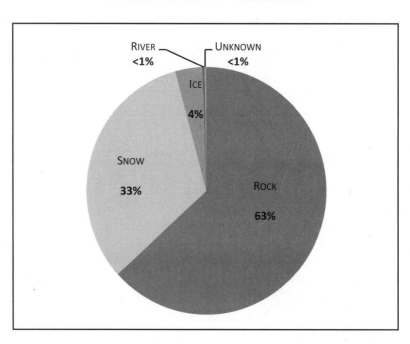

ACCIDENTS BY ASCENT VS. DESCENT

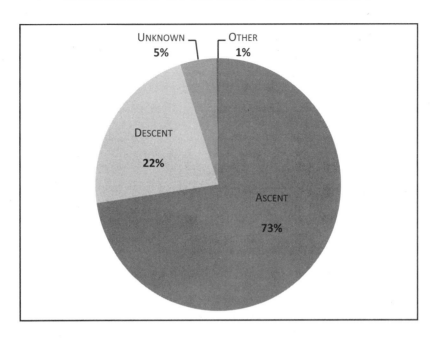

ACCIDENTS BY EXPERIENCE LEVEL

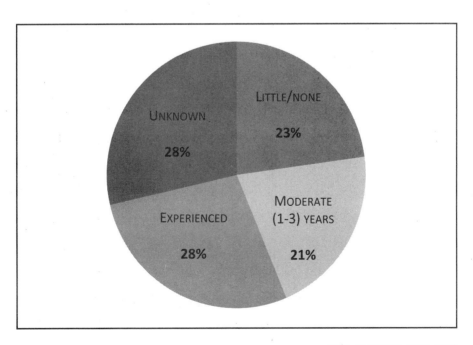

*USA Accidents, 1951–2012

MOUNTAIN RESCUE ASSOCIATION

P.O. Box 880868
San Diego, CA 92168-0868
www.mra.org

Doug Wessen, President
Juneau Mountain Rescue, Inc.
2970 Foster Ave.
Juneau, AK 99801
dougwessen@gmail.com
907-586-4834
Term Expires 2014

Dave Clarke, Vice President
42271 S. Coleman Road
Sandy, OR 97055
daveclarke@frontier.com
503-784-6341
Term Expires 2014

John Chang, Secretary/Treasurer
Bay Area Mountain Rescue
P.O. Box 19184
Stanford, CA 94309
sectreas@mra.org
925-699-2506 (cell)
Term Expires 2013

Bryan Enberg, Member-at-Large
3 Balanced Rock Terrace
Sparta, NJ 07871
bryan.enberg@gmail.com
973-459-0635 (cell)
Term Expires 2014

Jim Frank, Member-at-Large
Santa Barbara SAR Team
P.O. Box 6602
Santa Barbara, CA 93160
j.frank@impulse.net
805-961-1621 (w); 805-452-3261 (cell)
Term Expires 2013

Kayley Bell, Executive Secretary
P.O. Box 880868
San Diego, CA 92168
info@mra.org
858-229-4295 (h); 951-317-5635 (cell)